THE ROYAL COURT THEATRE PRESENTS

T0190818

the end of history...

by Jack Thorne

the end of history... was first performed at the Royal Court
Jerwood Theatre Downstairs, Sloane Square, on Thursday 27 June
2019.

the end of history...
by Jack Thorne

CAST (in order of appearance)

Polly **Kate O'Flynn**
Sal **Lesley Sharp**
David **David Morrissey**
Carl **Sam Swainsbury**
Harriet **Zoe Boyle**
Tom **Laurie Davidson**

Director **John Tiffany**
Designer **Grace Smart**
Lighting Designer **Jack Knowles**
Sound Designer **Tom Gibbons**
Movement Director **Steven Hoggett**
Casting Director **Amy Ball**
Production Manager **Marty Moore**
Costume Supervisor **Lucy Walshaw**
Assistant Director **Meghan Doyle**
Stage Manager **Kate Watkins**
Deputy Stage Manager **Sarah Hellicar**
Assistant Stage Manager **Crystal Gayle**
Stage Management Work Placement **Katie Stephen**
Set built by **Ridiculous Solutions**

The Quiet: written, composed, produced, engineered and mixed by **Imogen Heap**.
All rights Megaphonic Ltd, 2018.

The Royal Court & Stage Management wish to thank the following for their help with this production:
Jenny Grand at the Young Vic, Dr Rebecca E. Johnson, Lizzie for props,
Kevin from Killacleave Farm.

the end of history... is a recipient of the Edgerton Foundation New Play Award.

the end of history...
by Jack Thorne

Jack Thorne (Writer)

For the Royal Court: **Hope, Let the Right One In (& National Theatre of Scotland/West End/St Ann's, NYC).**

Other theatre includes: **Harry Potter and the Cursed Child (& West End), King Kong (Broadway); A Christmas Carol, Woyzeck (Old Vic); Junkyard (Headlong/Rose, Kingston/Bristol Old Vic/ Theatr Clwyd); The Solid Life of Sugar Water (Graeae/Edinburgh Festival Fringe/UK tour); The Borough (Punchdrunk/Aldeburgh Festival); Stuart: A Life Backwards [adaptation] (HighTide/Sheffield Theatres/Edinburgh Festival Fringe/UK tour); Mydidae (Drywrite/ Soho/West End); The Physicists [adaptation] (Donmar); Bunny (nabokov/Soho/59E59, NYC); 2nd May 1997 (& nabokov), Red Car Blue Car, Two Cigarettes, When You Cure Me (Bush); Greenland (National); Burying Your Brother in the Pavement (NT Connections); Stacy (Tron/ Arcola/West End); Fanny & Faggot (Pleasance, Edinburgh/Finborough/West End).**

Television includes: **The Virtues [co-writer], Kiri, National Treasure, The Last Panthers, Don't Take My Baby, This Is England [co-writer], The Fades, Glue, Cast-Offs.**

Film includes: **Wonder, War Book, A Long Way Down, The Scouting Book for Boys.**

Awards include: **Tony Award for Best Play, Olivier Award for Best New Play (Harry Potter and the Cursed Child); BAFTA for Best Mini-Series (National Treasure); BAFTA for Best Mini-Series (This Is England '90); BAFTA for Best Single Drama (Don't Take My Baby); BAFTA for Best Series (The Fades); BAFTA for Best Serial (This Is England '88).**

Zoe Boyle (Harriet)

For the Royal Court: **No Quarter.**

Other theatre includes: **Present Laughter (Theatre Royal, Bath/UK tour); Cat on a Hot Tin Roof (Leeds Playhouse); Six Degree of Separation (Old Vic); King Lear, The Seagull (RSC).**

Television includes: **Four Weddings & a Funeral, Witless, Frontier, The Astronaut Wives Club, Blandings, Breathless, Words of Everest, Bad Girls, Downton Abbey, Sons of Anarchy, Ghost Whisperer, Lewis: The Point of Vanishing, Poirot: An Appointment with Death.**

Film includes: **Sans Famille, La Promisse de L'aube, Freeloaders, King Lear.**

Laurie Davidson (Tom)

Theatre includes: **The Meeting (Chichester Festival); The Ferryman (West End).**

Television includes: **Will, Diana & I.**

Film includes: **Cats, The Good Liar.**

Meghan Doyle (Assistant Director)

As director, theatre includes: **To Kill a Mockingbird (NYT Rep); No Miracles Here (The Letter Room/ UK tour).**

As co-director, theatre includes: **Five Feet in Front: The Ballad of Little Johnny Wylo.**

As assistant director, theatre includes: **Macbeth, Victoria's Knickers, Consensual (NYT Rep); East is East (& Nottingham Playhouse), James & the Giant Peach (Northern Stage); Send More Paper (Camisado Club).**

Meghan is Co-Director of theatre company The Letter Room and was the recipient of the Bryan Forbes Assistant Director Award.

Tom Gibbons (Sound Designer)

For the Royal Court: **The Woods, Goats, Love Love Love.**

Other theatre includes: **All About Eve, Hamlet (& Almeida), Venus in Fur (West End); Hexenjagd (Theater Basel); The Wild Duck (Almeida); The Madness of George III (Nottingham Playhouse); Home I'm Darling (National/Theatr Clwyd); Fanny & Alexander, The Lorax (Old Vic); Oedipus (Toneelgroep, Amsterdam); Mr Burns, 1984 (& Broadway), Oresteia (Almeida/West End); A View from the Bridge (& West End), Life of Galileo, Happy Days, A Season in the Congo, Disco Pigs (Young Vic); Hedda Gabler, Sunset at the Villa Thalia, The Red Barn, People, Places & Things (National/West End); Les Misérables (Wermland Opera, Sweden); The Crucible (Broadway); Anna Karenina (Royal Exchange, Manchester); The Moderate Soprano, Elephants (Hampstead); White Devil, As You Like It (RSC); Translations, Plenty (Crucible, Sheffield); The Absence of War, Romeo & Juliet (Headlong); Lion Boy (Complicite); Henry IV, Julius Caesar (Donmar/St Ann's, NYC); Grounded (Gate); The Spire (Salisbury Playhouse); The Sound of Heavy Rain, The Initiate, Our Teacher's a Troll (& National Theatre of Scotland); Lungs, London, The Angry Brigade, Wasted (Paines Plough); The Rover (Hampton Court Palace); Dead Heavy Fantastic (Liverpool Everyman).**

Awards include: **Olivier Award for Best Sound Design (People, Places & Things).**

Steven Hoggett
(Movement Director)

For the Royal Court: **The Twits, Let the Right One In (& National Theatre of Scotland/West End/St Ann's, NYC).**

As movement director/choreographer, other theatre includes: **Harry Potter and the Cursed Child, The Curious Incident of the Dog in the Night-Time, Once (& West End), The Last Ship, Rocky: The Musical, The Glass Menagerie, American Idiot, Peter & the Starcatcher (Broadway); The Light Princess, 365, The Bacchae [& associate director], The Wolves in the Wall (& Improbable), Black Watch [& associate director] (National Theatre of Scotland); Mercury Fur, The Straits (Paines Plough).**

As director, other theatre includes: **Truth, War Correspondents (Helen Chadwick); What's It All About/Close To You: Bacharach Reimagined (New York Theatre Workshop/West End); Lovesong, Beautiful Burnout (& National Theatre of Scotland), Othello, Stockholm, pool (no water), Dirty Wonderland (Frantic Assembly).**

As choreographer, opera includes: **Rigoletto (Met, NYC); Dr Dee (ENO/Manchester International Festival).**

As director, opera includes: **Dalston Songs (ROH).**

As choreographer, film includes: **How To Train Your Dragon 2.**

Awards include: **Olivier Award for Best Theatre Choreographer (Black Watch); Lortel, Obie & Calloway Awards for Best Choreography (Once).**

Steven was Founder and Co-Artistic Director of Frantic Assembly. With Scott Graham, he co-wrote *The Frantic Assembly Book of Devising Theatre.*

Jack Knowles (Lighting Designer)

For the Royal Court: **Instructions for Correct Assembly, 2071.**

Other theatre includes: **Venice Preserved (RSC); Three Sisters, Shipwreck, Machinal, They Drink It in the Congo, Boy, Carmen Disruption, Game (Almeida); Top Girls, Cleansed (National); Caroline, or Change (Chichester Festival/Hampstead/West End); The Producers, Death of a Salesman, The Greatest Play in the History of the World, Happy Days, Parliament Square, Our Town, Twelfth Night, A Streetcar Named Desire, Wit, The Skriker, There Has Possibly Been An Incident (Royal Exchange, Manchester); Barber Shop Chronicles (National/Leeds Playhouse/Australia & US tours); Steel (Crucible, Sheffield); Good Vibrations (Lyric, Belfast); The Importance of Being Earnest (West End); Dan & Phil: Interactive Introverts,**
The Amazing Tour is Not on Fire (international tour); Circle Mirror Transformation (HOME, Manchester); Wonderland (Nottingham Playhouse/Northern Stage); Beginning (National/West End); Committee (Donmar); 4.48 Psychosis, Reisende auf einem Bein, Happy Days (Schauspielhaus, Hamburg); Junkyard, Pygmalion (Headlong); The Forbidden Zone (& Salzburg Festival/Barbican), Lungs, Yellow Wallpaper (Schaubühne, Berlin); The Massive Tragedy of Madame Bovary! (Liverpool Everyman/Peepolykus); The Haunting of Hill House (Liverpool Playhouse); Phaedra (Enniskillen International Beckett Festival); A Sorrow Beyond Dreams (Vienna Burgtheater); Moth (HighTide/Bush); Say It with Flowers (Hampstead); Night Train (Schauspiel, Köln/Avignon Festival/Theatertreffen).**

Awards include: **Knight of Illumination Award (Barber Shop Chronicles).**

David Morrissey (David)

For the Royal Court: **Hangmen (& West End).**

Other theatre includes: **Julius Caesar (Bridge); Macbeth (Liverpool Everyman); In a Dark Dark House (Almeida); Three Days of Rain (Donmar); Much Ado About Nothing (West End); Peer Gynt (National); King John, Henry VI, Edward IV, Richard III (RSC); The Cabinet Minister (Royal Exchange, Manchester); Ghetto (Riverside Studios); El Cid, Twelfth Night (Cheek by Jowl); Jug (Theatre Royal, Stratford East); WC/PC (Liverpool Playhouse).**

Television includes: **The Singapore Grip, Inside No.9, Britannia, The City & the City, The Missing, Extant, The Driver, The 7.39, The Walking Dead, True Love, London's Burning, Richard II, Field of Blood, South Riding, Scaredycat, Sleepyhead, Murder on the Orient Express, 5 Days, U Be Dead, The Red Riding Trilogy, Doctor Who, Sense & Sensibility, Cape Wrath, Ripley's Gold, Blackpool, The Deal, State of Play, Out of Control, Clocking Off, Murder, Pure Wickedness, Big Cat, Our Mutual Friend, Holding On, Out of the Blue, The One That Got Away, Available Light, Cause Celebre, One Summer.**

Film includes: **The Ones Below, Welcome to the Punch, Earthbound, Blitz, Nowhere Boy, Centurion, Mrs Mandela, Is Anybody There?, The Other Boleyn Girl, The Water Horse, The Reaping, Basic Instinct 2: Risk Addiction, Derailed, Stoned, This Little Life, Captain Corelli's Mandolin, Hilary & Jackie, Born Romantic, Card of Death, Fanny & Elvis, The Commissioner, Some Voices, Being Human, Waterland, Robin Hood, The Widow Maker, Drowning by Numbers.**

As director, film includes: **Bring Me Your Love (short), Sweet Revenge, Don't Worry About Me, Passerby, A Secret Audience (short).**

Awards include: **RTS Award for Best Actor (The Deal).**

Kate O'Flynn (Polly)

For the Royal Court: **Anatomy of a Suicide, The Ritual Slaughter of Gorge Mastromas, A Miracle.**

Other theatre includes: **One for the Road/Mountain Language/Ashes to Ashes (West End); The Glass Menagerie (West End/Edinburgh International Festival); The Trial (Young Vic); A Taste of Honey, Port (National); Lungs, The Sound of Heavy Rain (Paines Plough/Crucible, Sheffield); Marine Parade (ETT); The Whisky Taster (Bush); House of Special Purpose (Chichester Festival); See How They Run, The Children's Hour (Royal Exchange, Manchester).**

Television includes: **Brexit, No Offence, Wanderlust, Doctor Thorne, Not You Again, Ordinary Lies, New Tricks, Room at the Top, Playhouse Presents: The Snipist, Above Suspicion, The Syndicate, The Suspicions of Mr Whicher, Kingdom, The Palace, Trial & Retribution.**

Film includes: **Peterloo, Bridget Jones' Baby, Mr. Turner, Up There, Happy Go Lucky.**

Awards include: **Clarence Derwent Award for Best Female in a Supporting Role (The Glass Menagerie); Manchester Evening Standard Award for Best Newcomer, TMA Award for Best Supporting Actress (The Children's Hour); Critics' Circle Award for Most Promising Newcomer (Port).**

Lesley Sharp (Sal)

For the Royal Court: **The Woods, Ingredient X, Top Girls, The Recruiting Officer, Our Country's Good, Greenland, Road, Shirley, Gone, Who Knew McKenzie.**

Other theatre includes: **The Seagull (Lyric, Hammersmith); A Taste of Honey, Harper Regan, Mother Courage, Uncle Vanya, Murmuring Judges, Six Characters in Search of an Author, Fathers & Sons, Ting Tang Mine, True Dare Kiss, Command or Promise (National); Ghosts, Little Voice (West End); God of Hell, A Family Affair (Donmar); Mary & Lizzie, Playing with Trains (& RSC), Summerfolk (Chichester Festival).**

Television includes: **Living the Dream, Three Girls, Paranoid, Scott & Bailey, Capital, Starlings, The Shadow Line, Whistle & I'll Come to You, Cranford, Poirot, The Diary of Anne Frank, The Red Riding Trilogy, Doctor Who – Midnight, The Children, Afterlife, Planespotting, Carla, Carrie's War, The Second Coming, Bob & Rose, Clocking Off, Nature Boy, Great Expectations, Playing the Field, The Moonstone, Common as Muck, Prime Suspect, Dandelion Dead, Frank Stubbs, Road, Top Girls, Born with Two Mothers.**

Film includes: **Dusty & Me, Inkheart, Vera Drake, Cheeky, From Hell, The Full Monty, Naked, Priest, Close My Eyes, The Rachel Papers, Rita Sue & Bob Too, The Love Child.**

Awards include: **Sky Arts Television Award for Best Actress, Golden Nymph Award for Outstanding Actress in a Drama Series (Afterlife); Broadcasting Press Guild Award for Best Actress (Bob & Rose); Broadcasting Press Guild Award for Best Actress (Clocking Off); SAG Award for Outstanding Performance by a Cast (The Full Monty).**

Grace Smart (Designer)

Theatre includes: **My Beautiful Laundrette, Memoirs of an Asian Football Casual (Curve, Leicester); Crocodile Fever (Traverse); One Night in Miami, Shebeen (Nottingham Playhouse); God of Chaos (Theatre Royal, Plymouth); The Colleen Bawn (& Bruiser), St Joan, Good Vibrations [set], Here Comes the Night [set] (Lyric, Belfast); Killer Joe (West End); Postcards from the Ledge (Landmark Productions/Gaiety, Dublin); East is East (& Northern Stage), Mighty Atoms (Hull Truck); Normal, Blasted (STYX); Shopping & Fucking [costume] (Lyric, Hammersmith); Here Lie the Remains of Mercy (Theatre Deli); Wonderland [costume] (UK tour); Bar Mitzvah Boy (Gatehouse, Stafford); A Doll's House (Dissolve/The Space); Object Love (Dissolve/VAULT Festival); The Pier (Oxford Playhouse); The Picture of Dorian Gray [set], Three Sisters on Hope Street (LIPA).**

Opera includes: **The World's Wife (Mavron Quartet/WNO).**

As assistant designer, theatre includes: **Guys & Dolls (West End/UK tour); Splendour (Donmar); Our Country's Good (National); Seven Brides for Seven Brothers (Regent's Park Open Air); City Stories (St James); The White Wale (Slung Low); Macbeth (Manchester International Festival); La Tempesta (Scarabeus Aerial/Little Angel).**

Awards include: **Linbury Prize for Design (St Joan).**

Sam Swainsbury (Carl)

Theatre includes: **The Twilight Zone (Almeida); The Meeting (Hampstead); A Midsummer Night's Dream, Privates on Parade, When Did You Last See My Mother? (West End); Far from the Madding Crowd (Watermill); The Taming of the Shrew (RSC); The Comedy of Errors/Richard III, The Merchant of Venice/A Midsummer Night's Dream (Propeller); Hay Fever (Rose, Kingston); A Day at the Racists (Finborough); The Rivals (Southwark); Burial at Thebes (Nottingham Playhouse/Barbican); Hysteria (Birmingham Rep); Slope (Tramway, Glasgow).**

Television includes: **Victoria III, Fearless, Mum, Atlantis, Call the Midwife, Jekyll.**

Film includes: **Fisherman's Friends, The Cannibal in the Jungle, Thor: The Dark World.**

John Tiffany (Director)

For the Royal Court: **Road, The Twits, Hope, The Pass, Let the Right One In (& National Theatre of Scotland/West End/St Ann's, NYC).**

Other theatre includes: **Harry Potter and the Cursed Child, The Glass Menagerie, Once (Broadway/ West End); The Ambassador (BAM, NYC); Pinocchio (National); Enquirer, Macbeth, Peter Pan, The House of Bernarda Alba, Transform Caithness: Hunter, Be Near Me, Nobody Will Ever Forgive Us, The Bacchae, Black Watch, Elizabeth Gordon Quinn, Home: Glasgow (National Theatre of Scotland).**

Awards Include: **Tony & Olivier Awards for Best Director of a Play (Harry Potter and the Cursed Child); Sky Arts South Bank Show Award (Let the Right One In); Tony Award for Best Direction of a Musical (Once); Olivier Award for Best Director, Critics Circle Award for Best Director, Sky Arts South Bank Show Award (Black Watch).**

John is an Associate Director at the Royal Court. From 2010 to 2011 he was a Radcliffe Fellow at Harvard University.

THE ROYAL COURT THEATRE

The Royal Court Theatre is the writers' theatre. It is a leading force in world theatre for cultivating and supporting writers – undiscovered, emerging and established.

Through the writers, the Royal Court is at the forefront of creating restless, alert, provocative theatre about now. We open our doors to the unheard voices and free thinkers that, through their writing, change our way of seeing.

Over 120,000 people visit the Royal Court in Sloane Square, London, each year and many thousands more see our work elsewhere through transfers to the West End and New York, UK and international tours, digital platforms, our residencies across London, and our site-specific work. Through all our work we strive to inspire audiences and influence future writers with radical thinking and provocative discussion.

The Royal Court's extensive development activity encompasses a diverse range of writers and artists and includes an ongoing programme of writers' attachments, readings, workshops and playwriting groups. Twenty years of the International Department's pioneering work around the world means the Royal Court has relationships with writers on every continent.

Within the past sixty years, John Osborne, Samuel Beckett, Arnold Wesker, Ann Jellicoe, Howard Brenton and David Hare have started their careers at the Court. Many others including Caryl Churchill, Athol Fugard, Mark Ravenhill, Simon Stephens, debbie tucker green, Sarah Kane – and, more recently, Lucy Kirkwood, Nick Payne, Penelope Skinner and Alistair McDowall – have followed.

The Royal Court has produced many iconic plays from Lucy Kirkwood's **The Children** to Jez Butterworth's **Jerusalem** and Martin McDonagh's **Hangmen**.

Royal Court plays from every decade are now performed on stage and taught in classrooms and universities across the globe.

It is because of this commitment to the writer that we believe there is no more important theatre in the world than the Royal Court.

Supported using public funding by
ARTS COUNCIL ENGLAND

 royalcourt royalcourttheatre

ROYAL

COMING UP AT THE ROYAL COURT

4 - 27 Jul

seven methods of killing kylie jenner
By Jasmine Lee-Jones

Part of the Royal Court's Jerwood New Playwrights programme, supported by Jerwood Arts

3 – 21 Sep

Total Immediate Collective Imminent Terrestrial Salvation
By Tim Crouch

A National Theatre of Scotland production in association with the Royal Court Theatre, Teatro do Bairro Alto, Lisbon and Attenborough Centre for the Creative Arts (ACCA)

18 Sep – 12 Oct

Glass
Kill
Bluebeard
and
Imp
By Caryl Churchill

10 Oct – 16 Nov

A History of Water in the Middle East
By Sabrina Mahfouz

24 Oct – 23 Nov

On Bear Ridge
By Ed Thomas

National Theatre Wales and Royal Court Theatre

27 Nov – 21 Dec

Midnight Movie
By Eve Leigh

Part of the Royal Court's Jerwood New Playwrights programme, supported by Jerwood Arts

5 Dec – 18 Jan

A Kind of People
By Gurpreet Kaur Bhatti

royalcourttheatre.com

COURT

ROYAL

ASSISTED PERFORMANCES

Captioned Performances

Captioned performances are accessible for D/deaf, deafened & hard of hearing people as well as being suitable for people for whom English is not a first language. There are regular captioned performances in the Jerwood Theatre Downstairs on Wednesdays and the Jerwood Theatre Upstairs on Fridays.

In the Jerwood Theatre Downstairs
the end of history...: Wed 10, 17 (plus live speech-to-text post-show talk), 24, 31 Jul & 7 Aug, 7.30pm
Glass, Kill, Bluebeard, and Imp: Wed 2 & 9 Oct, 7.30pm
On Bear Ridge: Wed 6, 13, 20 & Fri 22 Nov, 7.30pm

In the Jerwood Theatre Upstairs
seven methods of killing kylie jenner: Fri 19 & 26 Jul, 7.45pm
Total Immediate Collective Imminent Terrestrial Salvation: Fri 13 & 20 Sep, 7.45pm
A History of Water in the Middle East: Fri 25 Oct, 1, 8 & 15 Nov, 7.45pm

Audio Described Performances

Audio described performances are accessible for blind or partially sighted customers. They are preceded by a touch tour (at 1pm) which allows patrons access to elements of theatre design including set & costume.

In the Jerwood Theatre Downstairs
the end of history...: Sat 3 Aug, 2.30pm
Glass, Kill, Bluebeard, and Imp: Sat 12 Oct, 2.30pm
On Bear Ridge: Sat 23 Nov, 2.30pm

Midnight Movie
Jerwood Theatre Upstairs
Wed 27 Nov – Sat 21 Dec
The production will creatively combine Spoken English, BSL, captioning and audio description.
Please contact our Box Office for more information.

ROYAL

ASSISTED PERFORMANCES

Performances in a Relaxed Environment

Relaxed Environment performances are suitable for those who may benefit from a more relaxed experience.

During these performances:
- There will be a relaxed attitude to noise in the auditorium; you are welcome to respond to the show in whatever way feels natural
- You can enter and exit the auditorium when needed
- We will help you find the best seats
- House lights remained raised slightly

In the Jerwood Theatre Downstairs
the end of history...: Sat 27 Jul, 2.30pm
Glass, Kill, Bluebeard, and Imp: Sat 5 Oct, 2.30pm
On Bear Ridge: Sat 16 Nov, 2.30pm
A Kind of People: Sat 11 Jan, 2.30pm
Poet in da Corner: Sat 8 Feb, 2.30pm

In the Jerwood Theatre Upstairs
Total Immediate Collective Imminent Terrestrial Salvation:
Sat 21 Sep, 3pm
A History of Water in the Middle East: Sat 9 Nov, 3pm
Midnight Movie: All shows will be performed in a relaxed environment.
Wed 27 Nov – Sat 21 Dec.
Scenes with Girls: Sat 15 Feb, 3pm

If you would like to talk to us about your access requirements please contact our Box Office at (0)20 7565 5000 or **boxoffice@royalcourttheatre.com.**
A Royal Court Visual Story is available on our website. We also produce a Story Synopsis & Sensory Synopsis which are available on request.

For more information and to book access tickets online, visit

royalcourttheatre.com/assisted-performances

Sloane Square London, SW1W 8AS ⊖ Sloane Square ⇌ Victoria Station
🐦 royalcourt 📘 royalcourttheatre

COURT

ROYAL COURT SUPPORTERS

The Royal Court is a registered charity and not–for–profit company. We need to raise £1.5 million every year in addition to our core grant from the Arts Council and our ticket income to achieve what we do.

We have significant and longstanding relationships with many generous organisations and individuals who provide vital support. Royal Court supporters enable us to remain the writers' theatre, find stories from everywhere and create theatre for everyone.

We can't do it without you.

PUBLIC FUNDING

Arts Council England, London
British Council

TRUSTS & FOUNDATIONS

The Backstage Trust
The Bryan Adams Charitable Trust
The Austin & Hope Pilkington Trust
The Boshier-Hinton Foundation
Martin Bowley Charitable Trust
The Chapman Charitable Trust
Gerald Chapman Fund
CHK Charities
The City Bridge Trust
The Cleopatra Trust
The Clifford Chance Foundation
Cockayne - Grants for the Arts
The Ernest Cook Trust
The Nöel Coward Foundation
Cowley Charitable Trust
Edgerton Foundation
The Eranda Rothschild Foundation
Lady Antonia Fraser for The Pinter Commission
Genesis Foundation
The Golden Bottle Trust
The Haberdashers' Company
The Paul Hamlyn Foundation
Roderick & Elizabeth Jack
Jerwood Arts
The Leche Trust
The Andrew Lloyd Webber Foundation
The London Community Foundation
John Lyon's Charity
Clare McIntyre's Bursary
Old Possum's Practical Trust
The David & Elaine Potter Foundation
The Richard Radcliffe Charitable Trust
Rose Foundation
Royal Victoria Hall Foundation
The Sobell Foundation
Span Trust
John Thaw Foundation
The Garfield Weston Foundation

CORPORATE SPONSORS

American Express
Aqua Financial Solutions Ltd
Cadogan
Colbert
Edwardian Hotels, London
Fever-Tree
Gedye & Sons
Green Rooms
Greene King
Kirkland & Ellis International LLP
Kudos
MAC

CORPORATE MEMBERS

Platinum
Lombard Odier

Gold
Weil, Gotshal & Manges LLP

Silver
Auerbach & Steele Opticians
Bloomberg
Kekst CNC
Left Bank Pictures
The No 8 Partnership Dental Practice
PATRIZIA
Royal Bank of Canada - Global Asset Management
Tetragon Financial Group
Wilde Ones

For more information or to become a foundation or business supporter contact: support@royalcourttheatre. com/020 7565 5064.

Supported using public funding by
ARTS COUNCIL
ENGLAND

ROYAL
BAR & KITCHEN

The Royal Court's Bar & Kitchen aims to create a welcoming and inspiring environment with a style and ethos that reflects the work we put on stage. Our menu consists of simple, ingredient driven and flavour-focused dishes with an emphasis on freshness and seasonality. This is supported by a carefully curated drinks list notable for its excellent wine selection, craft beers and skilfully prepared coffee. By day a perfect spot for long lunches, meetings or quiet reflection and by night an atmospheric, vibrant meeting space for cast, crew, audiences and the general public.

GENERAL OPENING HOURS
Monday – Friday: 10am – late
Saturday: 12noon – late

Advance booking is suggested at peak times.

For more information, visit
royalcourttheatre.com/bar

HIRES & EVENTS

The Royal Court is available to hire for celebrations, rehearsals, meetings, filming, ceremonies and much more. Our two theatre spaces can be hired for conferences and showcases, and the building is a unique venue for bespoke weddings and receptions.

For more information, visit
royalcourttheatre.com/events

Sloane Square London, SW1W 8AS ⊖ Sloane Square ⇌ Victoria Station
🐦 royalcourt 📘 royalcourttheatre

"There are no spaces, no rooms in my opinion, with a greater legacy of fearlessness, truth and clarity than this space."
Simon Stephens, Associate Playwright

The Royal Court invests in the future of the theatre, offering writers the support, time and resources to find their voices and tell their stories, asking the big questions and responding to the issues of the moment.

As a registered charity, the Royal Court needs to raise at least £1.5 million every year in addition to our Arts Council funding and ticket income, to keep seeking out, developing and nurturing new voices. Please join us by donating today.

You can donate online at **royalcourttheatre.com/donate** or via our **donation box in the Bar & Kitchen.**

We can't do it without you.

Support the Court

To find out more about the different ways in which you can be involved please contact support@royalcourttheatre.com/ 020 7565 5049

The English Stage Company at the Royal Court Theatre is a registered charity (No. 231242).

the end of history...

Jack Thorne

For Maggie, Mike, Jo, Chris and Liz.
With love.

'And drops on gate-bars hang in a row,
And rooks in families homeward go,
And so do I.'

Thomas Hardy

Characters

POLLY, *nineteen, twenty-nine and thirty-nine*
SAL, *forty-six and fifty-six*
DAVID, *fifty-one, sixty-one and seventy-one*
CARL, *twenty, thirty and forty*
HARRIET, *twenty-one and thirty-one*
TOM, *seventeen, twenty-seven and thirty-seven*

There are ten years between each of the acts and they take place in the winter of 1997, the summer of 2007 and the spring of 2017.

All the action takes place in a family home in Newbury, Berkshire.

This text went to press before the end of rehearsals and so may differ slightly from the play as performed.

ACT ONE

1997.

A slightly overstuffed dining room–kitchen. There are family pictures on every wall and artefacts from Sierra Leone, Hong Kong and Indonesia.

There are casually treated and well-read books everywhere as well as the occasional stack of correspondence or the odd interesting ripped-out article from a newspaper.

There's also some dust.

POLLY *is dressed in black,* SAL *is in a plastic checkered apron.*

POLLY. What I resent is being given no choice in the matter.

SAL. You have a choice. You can sleep on the sofa, or on your brother's floor.

POLLY. I just don't see why I...

SAL. It's the nicest room.

POLLY. It's the nicest room because *I made it* the nicest room.

SAL. We want her to feel comfortable.

POLLY. And you're happy for your daughter to feel uncomfortable?

Beat.

SAL. If it was up to us, they'd share a bed, we don't care if they want to fool around...

POLLY *laughs.*

POLLY. Fool around?

SAL. Fuck. We don't care if they want to fuck. But both of them gave their words to her parents and feel obliged to stick to those words.

POLLY. Religious?

SAL. Catholic.

POLLY. Really?

SAL. Ya-huh.

POLLY. And just to be clear – you would have them betray her parents' trust?

SAL. All the best children do I've heard. Besides, I believe their parents' beliefs are based on a false construct that might ultimately damage her.

POLLY. Beware false idols.

Beat. SAL isn't sure if that's a dig.

Why can't she sleep in Tom's room?

SAL. Because it smells of dirty socks and dirty magazines and I can't seem to be able to eradicate either.

POLLY. Why can't she sleep in Carl's room and he sleep on the sofa?

SAL. Because then she'll get embarrassed and insist she sleep on the sofa and your father will walk through with nothing on for his morning coffee and cause her a fright.

POLLY. I don't want to sleep on the sofa.

SAL. And if she hasn't seen the male naked form before then I'd rather the first not be your father's. It might put her off for life. You can share with us if you'd like?

POLLY. What?

SAL. Me. Share with me. I could kick David out – make him sleep on the sofa – and we could share a bed. You and I, I mean.

POLLY. No.

SAL. It's a new mattress. We just got a new mattress. It's wonderful, it's like sleeping on a – what would be the appropriate metaphor?

POLLY. I don't know.

SAL. We never have sex any more because we don't want to damage the springs and sleeping is too nice.

POLLY *looks at her.*

Nothing makes me happier than oversharing with you. Your lip literally disappears inside yourself it gets so thin.

Beat.

You left home.

POLLY. I went to university.

SAL. The room is no longer your possession. It's ours. And we want your brother's girlfriend to be comfortable. If you had brought home a boyfriend and your brother didn't have anyone –

POLLY. Didn't have anyone. Nice.

SAL. I would say that he should be kicked out so your – imaginary boyfriend – could have his room.

She smiles at her daughter, who reluctantly smiles back.

POLLY. Thanks.

SAL. Oh darling, I'm kidding you, you'll have plenty of boyfriends, you probably have one now, you just won't want to tell me because I'll embarrass you with over-intrusive questions.

POLLY. You're right, I have several.

SAL. Long as they're not economics students.

POLLY. They're not.

SAL. I've no problem with their intellectual aspirations – if they want to be economists – let them be economists – but, in my experience, they tend to be perverts.

POLLY. Yup. You've already said.

SAL. I dated two – I think out of an anthropological desire to understand economists if not economics – and it was the age of Keynes as king so not quite so – you know, neither were driven by money – most of them want to be in the city I imagine in your year – anyway, I digress, both tried for anal sex. Both of them. And they were really affronted when I wouldn't let them.

POLLY *is just staring at her mum.*

You see – lovely curled lip again – you actually have lovely
lips – you take after David's mum. I'd love lovely lips like
you've got.

POLLY. I'm going to get dressed for dinner.

SAL. I try to teach all my students about – when we do Dickens
– about the price mechanism – never accept a cinema ticket
from a boy unless you're prepared to, I don't know, wank
them off after – nothing's free in this world – perhaps I let
them buy me too many drinks. The economists.

POLLY. Perhaps. Okay. Dressed.

SAL. You're not wearing that?

POLLY. No.

SAL. But you look really nice.

POLLY. I have no idea how your students survive your Dickens
class.

SAL. No.

POLLY. You don't really talk about wanking?

SAL. I'd be fired if I talked about wanking. I imply wanking. And
I'm doing them a favour, aren't I? They need to learn about
patriarchal capitalism from someone. It's surprisingly low-cut
for daywear. If you have a different outfit for – nightwear.

Beat.

POLLY. Don't worry, Mum, for dinner, I'm wearing a blouse
with buttons all the way up to my mouth. I don't want to
scare her with unnecessary skin. Okay. See you.

SAL. You know her parents own most of Hampshire.

POLLY. Oh, I see...

SAL. You don't.

POLLY. That is why you've given her the best room. Deference.

SAL. No. Come on.

POLLY. And here was I worrying you were going to upset her
by saying something political, now I'm worrying that you'll
embarrass her through bowing too deep. And they don't own

most of Hampshire, they own a series of hotels, the largest of which is in Hampshire.

SAL. I'm just excited he's found someone so interesting.

POLLY. And they're big in service stations apparently. Your fascination with people with money...

SAL. Don't mistake fascination for approval. Has he always gone for girls like – that?

POLLY *gives* SAL *her best sardonic smile.*

POLLY. Has he always gone for posh girls?

SAL. Bit crude but I guess that's the question I'm asking.

POLLY. Yes, he used to hang around St Gabriel's with his tongue hanging out.

SAL. Really?

POLLY. When we'd go to the Waterside centre, he'd stalk anyone in a boater.

SAL. He used to hate going there with you.

POLLY. Probably I'm lying then. Can I go now?

SAL. Can we share a bed? Can I kick your father out? Can we share a bed? I'd really like that.

POLLY. Am I going to wake up at three in the morning and find you spooning me?

SAL. Maybe.

POLLY *grins.*

POLLY. Yeah. Okay. We can share a bed. Better than the sofa.

SAL *looks at her.*

SAL. I have missed you so much, you do know that, don't you?

POLLY. Sure.

SAL. No one to write my Amnesty letters with.

POLLY. Okay. Really? That's what you miss?

SAL. No one to do the gardening with.

POLLY. I gave up on that a long time ago.

SAL. Your father has too. Missed you too.

POLLY. Okay.

SAL. Our extraordinary daughter back from her extraordinary university.

POLLY. Much more ordinary than you think, Sal.

She exits.

SAL *is left.*

She looks after her.

She retreats to the stove, she tests the pots. She adds more salt.

DAVID *walks into the room.*

DAVID. Don't talk to me, I need to keep a thought in my head.

SAL. Potatoes and cucumber.

DAVID. Bugger off.

SAL. Fox fur.

DAVID. Shit bag.

SAL. *101 Dalmatians.*

DAVID. Jesus.

He picks up the newspaper. He exits.

SAL *turns on the radio.*

RADIO 4. Tony Blair announced today –

SAL turns the radio off.

SAL. No.

She jiggles around a little bit.

She thinks and then adds more salt to the pots.

After a beat she adds more curry powder.

DAVID *re-enters.*

DAVID. He's here. I saw him down the street.

SAL. From where?

DAVID. The toilet.

SAL. What thought did you need to keep in your head on the toilet?

DAVID. She looks nice.

SAL. How do I look?

DAVID. The lady has a casual intellect with an easy style underneath which sits a body that is still in remarkable shape for her years.

SAL. Spoilt that by saying 'for her years' at the end.

DAVID. Ah. Schoolboy error.

SAL. And surprising for a man of your years.

DAVID. Ha!

SAL. Blair's announced something again.

DAVID. What?

SAL. I don't know. I couldn't listen to it.

DAVID. You think that's the answer?

SAL. I think that's an answer. Gerry called – he wants to know if we can help with the nurses' fête on Saturday.

DAVID. Can we?

SAL. I said yes.

DAVID. Okay. Well. Okay.

   DAVID *looks at her.*

SAL. I'll sell some of our pot plants, you do the tombola.

DAVID. I'm not going anywhere near that fucking tombola.

SAL. You sell the pot plants then and I'll be on the fucking tombola. Don't look at me like that.

   DAVID *looks at her like that again.*

DAVID. Whatever you're nervous about…

SAL. I'm not nervous about anything. I'm excited.

DAVID. Tonight will be fine.

SAL. St Gabriel's is the girls' school isn't it?

DAVID. Yes. Private. Very expensive. Alan threatened to send his daughter there for sixth form – don't you remember? You staged a walkout of quiz night.

SAL. That's not true.

DAVID. I remember it clearly.

SAL. I politely left.

DAVID. Polly being tricky?

SAL. Says I'm salivating over this girl because she's rich –

DAVID. Salivating?

SAL. My word. Accused me of deference.

DAVID. Total true deference. Is it true you cleaned?

SAL. Oh fuck off.

DAVID. Do we know what time Tom is going to be here?

SAL. Tom Tom Tom.

DAVID. Oh.

The doorbell rings.

I'll answer it. You'll embarrass her by curtsying on the doorstep.

SAL. Oh, you're sleeping on the sofa tonight.

DAVID. Am I?

SAL. Polly's coming in with me.

DAVID. So I defer to Polly in order so you can defer to Harriet. I smell impending revolution.

SAL. She's already told me I'm not allowed to spoon her. Do you know what spooning is? I had to get a sixth-former to explain it in class to me once.

Beat.

We were doing Martin Amis I think. Do they spoon in Martin Amis?

DAVID. I'm going to answer the door.

He exits. And then he re-enters.

Don't listen to Polly – but do be gentle with her.

SAL. I'll try.

DAVID nods and exits. She checks the pots again.

She picks up a knife and checks her teeth and then her hair in the reflection of the blade.

She tries to do something with her hair – she's disappointed by whatever she does.

DAVID. And this is where the magic happens...

HARRIET. Hello.

CARL. Hi, Mother.

SAL kisses CARL and then hugs him. She looks at HARRIET as she does.

SAL. He normally calls me Sal, so that's for you.

CARL. Two seconds. That's how long it took her to contradict me, two seconds.

SAL. He called me Mum for a bit when he was embarrassed by Sal – but Mother is a whole new –

CARL. Say hello.

SAL. You must be Harriet. Has he told you his parents are hideously embarrassing?

CARL. Yup.

SAL. I'm going to try and behave. You're very welcome, Harriet. Has anyone offered to take your coat or similar?

HARRIET. That's not [necessary].

SAL. David, take her coat.

DAVID. Okay. I'll hang it on the stairs. We don't have a special cupboard or anything.

HARRIET. That's okay.

DAVID takes her coat.

SAL. What a lovely outfit.

HARRIET. Is it? Thank you.

CARL. It's nice. You look nice. Great.

SAL. That's – impressive. You've trained him already.
  Congratulations on that –

CARL. Mum –

SAL. That's the first time I've heard him compliment anyone or
  anything in at least five years. Though it is a nice dress.
  Complements you. Shows you – off. Et cetera.

CARL. Mum, stop…

SAL. Stop what? Stop talking. If I stop talking, no one will say
  anything. Where's your dad gone?

CARL. I don't – know.

There's a silence.

HARRIET. This is a lovely place.

SAL. Newbury or the house?

HARRIET. Sorry.

SAL. What place were you referring to?

HARRIET. This – house…

CARL. She meant the house, Mum.

SAL. Well, yes, well, it does. When we were in Manchester we
  lived somewhere with a bit more of an interesting history to
  it, but it does. The roof fits. Et cetera.

There's an awkward silence.

  Now, he's told us nothing about you.

CARL. And so it begins.

SAL. Can you stop?

CARL. What?

SAL. Can you stop being – stop being – you…

CARL. I – I am not being me – I'm being – Jesus, Mum.

  SAL *turns to* HARRIET.

SAL. Do you mind if I ask some questions, Harriet?

CARL. Do you mind if I mind you asking questions, Mum?

SAL. What does your mum do?

HARRIET. As in – work? She doesn't.

DAVID *re-enters. He sits on the sofa. He opens a newspaper.*

SAL. She's a stay-at-home mum.

HARRIET. Well, she does some charity work. But a lot of – we have dogs, you know… lots to do. But yes, she stays at home.

CARL. She cooks and everything.

SAL. What charity work?

HARRIET. I don't really – know –

SAL. Oh.

HARRIET. Horses. I think. Something to do with horses. She's not that involved – mainly it's the dogs.

SAL. And your dad's a hotelier?

HARRIET. Sort of. There's a family business.

SAL. Service stations too I hear. How does someone own service stations? I'm fascinated.

HARRIET. I don't really – it doesn't really interest me.

SAL. But do you own the – the petrol station, the – facilities – the, I don't know, Little Chef?

CARL. Little Chef?

HARRIET. I believe Little Chef is a franchise. We rent to them.

SAL. I never thought of it as a rental.

CARL. I don't think Little Chef is that much – I don't even think there's that many – how many Little Chefs are there?

SAL. Used to be our treat – whenever we went on holiday – we'd get up early – to beat the traffic and stop for breakfast in a Little Chef.

CARL. I liked the pancakes.

SAL. And the ice cream.

She pats his belly. He retracts away.

I always admired the people who worked there. In them. So crucial. That they're well run. That they're – you know – for lorry drivers I mean. They're – well, I suppose, islands in a storm I suppose, for so many.

HARRIET. I don't know much about them. They're just –

SAL. Part of the business. So to speak.

CARL. Mum, maybe we could...

SAL. Am I interrogating? Fuck. I thought I was conversing. Sorry. Harriet.

HARRIET. I don't mind.

CARL. I do.

SAL. No, it's my talent I'm afraid, no talent at all when it comes to cooking – as you will discover – but when it comes to pissing off my children – immense talent – Olympian talent. I'm sure your mum – mother is much more – decorous.

CARL. Decorous.

SAL. Can you stop it, Carl, please?

Beat.

So I imagine you've travelled the world...

HARRIET. Um...

SAL. That's what we'd do if I had money. Travel the world. See the – sights.

HARRIET. We don't have that much money.

SAL. Then you should up Little Chef's rent.

HARRIET. Well...

SAL. I suspect the minimum wage will be creating some problems for you though.

CARL. Mum –

HARRIET. I honestly wouldn't –

SAL. But then there's the changes to pension tax relief, that must –

CARL. Mum. This is not our [business].

HARRIET. I don't really have much to do with what Daddy –
Dad – my father does.

SAL. But aren't you fascinated? David and I have always made
the kids take an interest.

CARL. Dad used to read his credit-card bills out loud to us. It
was fascinating.

DAVID *lowers his paper.*

DAVID. I apologise for boring you.

CARL. It was actually how I found out there was no Father
Christmas. Dad read a bill with all our presents on.

POLLY. Sorry I'm late.

POLLY *is in quite a low-cut dress.*

Sorry. Hello, Carlio. Hello, Harriet. I'm Sister Polly.

HARRIET. Hi.

POLLY. I'm guessing she's already fired at least three atom
bombs by now?

CARL. Hydrogen. She went big. Wiped out most of Europe and
not a small part of China.

SAL. I was just having an interesting conversation.

POLLY. Yup.

DAVID *lowers his paper.*

DAVID. We are excited to have you here, Harriet.

HARRIET. Okay. Thank you.

DAVID. Carl's never brought a girl home before and he's
beginning to wish he didn't now.

CARL. Thanks, Dad.

HARRIET. Yeah. Okay.

POLLY. Helpful, Dad.

DAVID. We're all amazed you've got two legs and a mouth.

HARRIET. What did you think I'd look like?

DAVID. Oh, you wouldn't want to know.

CARL. Three heads.

POLLY. Seven arms.

CARL. And no bottom whatsoever.

HARRIET. What?

CARL. Doesn't matter.

DAVID. No. I guess not.

> DAVID *raises his paper back up. The conversation is over.*
> HARRIET *frowns and says nothing.*

SAL. Sit down. Everyone sit down.

CARL. Where's Tommy?

SAL. On his way. He had to stay late at school.

CARL. Why?

POLLY. What's he done this time?

SAL (*dry*). Some sort of civil disobedience I'm guessing wouldn't you? Either that or drugs.

CARL. Okay.

SAL. My youngest son was thrown off the school history trip this year, did Carl already tell you?

HARRIET. Yeah.

SAL. He was dealing hash amongst the other boys. We thought – being caught – might lead to a change of attitude, and we tried to help him through that, but it hasn't. The only problem is – sit down, I need to check on the curry.

> *She takes a spoonful of the curry and then a spoonful of the rice. She spits the rice into a piece of hastily acquired kitchen roll.*

HARRIET. I like curry.

SAL. You won't like mine. The problem is university. How it affects his university choices. If you don't get into a first-rate university it – well, in today's job market, et cetera et cetera...

> *The kids sit.*

Well, the curry's done but the rice definitely needs
simmering time. I'll put the naan in.

HARRIET. I like naan.

SAL. Are you joining us, David?

DAVID. Just finishing this article on education in jails. They're
being stymied by their promise to meet Tory funding targets.

SAL. You see?

*She pulls some naan out of packets and puts them in the oven
before sitting down.*

DAVID. Guess the level of reoffending in this country – guess
the likelihood of leaving jail and then coming more or less
straight back –

SAL. I don't know.

DAVID. Guess.

She gets up again and turns on the oven.

SAL. Within what time period?

DAVID. The reoffending?

He checks through the paper.

It doesn't say so I guess infinite time period.

SAL. Thirty-five per cent.

DAVID. Polly?

POLLY. Forty-five.

DAVID. Carl?

CARL. Forty-four.

POLLY. Still a dick.

CARL. Always.

DAVID. Harriet, you want to hazard an answer?

HARRIET. I wouldn't – know –

DAVID. Guess.

HARRIET. I couldn't.

DAVID. Sixty per cent. If you leave jail you are more likely to return to jail than do anything else. And in jail education services –

SAL. Despite Blair's promises –

DAVID. Is not getting the money or support they need. They need to be pumping money in. It doesn't make economic or social sense to do otherwise.

CARL. Easy though – to find a way to criticise him for not living up to every value –

SAL. Shouldn't he live up to his values?

CARL. He was elected as a pragmatic social democrat – you even voted for him, Mum, and you were well aware of his faults.

SAL. I voted for my local Labour candidate, Paul Hannon, and he always speaks marvellously and I think – though wouldn't like to speak on his behalf – would reject the label of pragmatic.

CARL. This was Newbury, it didn't matter what he said, he wasn't going to get elected.

SAL. Yes. Yes. The tragedy of our lives. Despite the Greenham women. Have you heard of the Greenham women, Harriet?

HARRIET. Yes.

CARL. Of course she has. Well, anyway, Pol won, she was closest.

POLLY. I'd like to thank my family, the books I've read, I'd like to thank the television – particularly Channel 4 news –

SAL *checks the oven.*

SAL. It's not heating up again.

DAVID *walks over to investigate the oven.*

DAVID. You probably didn't press the hoo-ha again.

SAL. David, you have to save me, the naan will be the only edible bit of the meal.

Beat.

So you're going into your third year, Harriet?

HARRIET. Yeah.

DAVID *twists a knob on the oven. He stands holding his hand to it.*

SAL. Of a degree in French?

HARRIET. Yeah.

SAL. What does one do with a degree in French?

HARRIET *looks at* CARL.

CARL. Ethically, politically, pragmatically or personally?

POLLY *laughs.*

SAL. For a job. What do you do for a job? Or are you planning to work in the family business –

DAVID *removes the tray of naan and puts his head inside the oven.*

CARL. She's still working it out –

HARRIET. I don't quite – know –

CARL. There's a lot of work in industrial translation.

DAVID *removes his head from the oven and returns with a packet of matches. He lights a match and puts his head back into the oven.*

SAL. Fascinating. Harriet, maybe you can talk me through it.

HARRIET. You translate documents for industry. Maybe car companies.

SAL. Okay. Great. What kind of documents? Sales documents? David, take your head out of the oven.

HARRIET. More – trade agreements – you might want to buy – I don't know – French tyres. And you – as you make the deal with them – so you hire me to translate all the documents –

SAL. And I'm sure your father could make use of that –

HARRIET. His work isn't really – he's not that interested in France…

DAVID *removes his head from the oven.*

DAVID. Nor was Henry V before Agincourt. The back bit wasn't igniting. It's on now.

SAL. Neither Polly or Carl have decided what to do either.

DAVID *puts the tray of naan into the oven. Then he checks the rice. He spits it out onto some kitchen roll.*

POLLY. I'm in my second year, Mum, so…

CARL. And I've actually decided I'm going to become a Greenham woman.

POLLY. That's not even funny.

SAL. David. Sit down.

DAVID *does.* SAL *looks at* HARRIET *with a smile.*

When I was your age I wanted to be in a band and sleep with Mick Jagger – and Jimi Hendrix – preferably together – so who am I to judge your choices. Will you have to travel to France? For work? Harriet?

HARRIET. I think so.

SAL. Or would you want to live in France and commute to England?

HARRIET. I don't know.

DAVID *gets up again and goes to look at the hobs.*

SAL. Carl used to be quite capable in French.

CARL. Mais oui.

SAL. David…

DAVID. Just trying to work out if there was a way of speeding up the rice.

SAL. Curry is okay, Harriet?

HARRIET. I already said. Great.

SAL. I like curry because it allows you to mask your mistakes. I use paste. Or jars. Do you have curries at home?

HARRIET. No.

SAL. More traditional – meat and two veg?

HARRIET. My mum likes Italian food.

SAL. We once went on holiday – to Normandy – and had Carl be the family's translator and he did very well, didn't he, Polly?

POLLY. Mais oui.

CARL. Mais oui. Mais oui.

SAL. It could be exciting to live in Paris together. Discover the city.

DAVID. Discover if the spirit of '68 lives on.

HARRIET. Spirit of '68?

POLLY. Student revolutions. Do you spot a running theme in this household yet?

SAL. Not just students. It could be fun. The bakeries are sensational. The wine – oooh la la. And Lionel Jospin is quite quite wonderful of course.

CARL. Sal, it's genuinely not your business where we live.

SAL. No. No. Of course not. I wasn't meaning... was I interfering?

POLLY. Were you interfering?

SAL *looks at* POLLY, *hurt*.

DAVID. Maybe we should move to Paris. Maybe the rice cooks faster there.

SAL. Polly, you talk for a bit.

POLLY *looks at* SAL.

Tell her about your degree, I don't know, I'm aware I'm talking too much and I'm choosing to absent myself from conversation. From now on. For a little while.

There's a silence. HARRIET *looks up*.

CARL. She does this.

HARRIET. You're at Oxford right?

POLLY. Cambridge.

HARRIET. Oh. Right. I applied to Oxford. They didn't take me.

POLLY. You probably did well to avoid it.

CARL. Aye.

HARRIET. What do you study?

POLLY. Law.

HARRIET. Do you want to be a solicitor or a barrister?

POLLY. My mum and dad want me to be Helena Kennedy.

HARRIET. The name rings a bell...

DAVID. Michael Bettany, Brighton Bombing, Guildford Four, Israeli Embassy bombing. Wonderful woman.

HARRIET. I'll have to look her up. So – barrister then?

POLLY. Maybe.

HARRIET. What's it like – there? Cambridge?

POLLY. Stuffy. Mildly depressed.

HARRIET. Depressed?

CARL. You're going to get her started.

POLLY. The problem with Cambridge is that everyone that goes there is defined by their intelligence. At school – I was the clever one –

CARL. She felt persecuted.

POLLY. Everyone would compare their grades to mine. I was the swot.

DAVID. You weren't just academic, you were also in the choir.

CARL. Sure, Dad. That's how it works. She was known as the Contralto.

POLLY. Then I get to Cambridge and suddenly I'm bang average.

CARL. Actually I quite like Contralto – can I call you Contralto now? I tried to start a nickname for her – at school – Pol Pot. Didn't stick.

POLLY. So I go from being defined as – to suddenly – I'm not defined by anything.

DAVID. You're hugely clever.

POLLY. And my journey is the typical one. Everyone's depressed there. Because they're not remarkable and they thought they were.

DAVID. Because they're not remarkable?

POLLY. Yes.

DAVID. But they're all remarkable. I would have given my back teeth to go to Cambridge.

POLLY. But you didn't have the chance, because you did not grow up with the same opportunities...

DAVID. Are you scoffing at me?

POLLY. No, Dad.

CARL. I wanted to go to Cambridge too. I had exactly the same opportunities.

POLLY. You wouldn't have wanted to be there.

DAVID. Of course he would – listen, Polly, all this – it's a remarkable excuse.

POLLY. What's a remarkable excuse?

CARL. Can everyone stop saying remarkable?

DAVID. For not achieving anything, for not attempting to stand out, it's a remarkable excuse.

POLLY. Yeah?

DAVID. Those who claim themselves average are the ones who then give themselves licence to behave in an average manner.

SAL (*firmly*). Okay.

DAVID *looks at his wife. He nods. He withdraws.*

POLLY. You seem to have started talking again, Sal.

SAL. Yes. I can but apologise.

There's a silence. DAVID *can't resist filling it.*

DAVID. There was a time when you didn't say 'my parents want me to be Helena Kennedy' – there was a time when you used to say – shyly – have you heard of Helena Kennedy – ? I want to be her.

POLLY. I can't remember that.

DAVID. Then you've a piss-poor memory.

SAL. I don't think getting angry at each other helps –

POLLY. First day of college, David drives me up…

DAVID. Are we really revisiting this?

POLLY. Harriet might be interested.

DAVID. Harriet probably wants to do nothing more than leave this house and run toward Hampshire.

CARL. True.

HARRIET. I don't live in Hampshire.

POLLY. First day of college David drives me in, there's a note waiting for me.

HARRIET. We just have a hotel there.

POLLY. Dean's tea party in the old library for students and parents. 3 p.m. We go of course. Five minutes in –

DAVID. I'd checked you were okay.

POLLY. Five minutes in David comes up to me and says 'I'm leaving.'

DAVID. You didn't need me around.

POLLY. Do you know why? Because someone had asked him what school I went to and he couldn't decide whether to wear my comprehensive-school education with pride or shame.

DAVID. She made perfectly fucking clear you wouldn't fit in and I didn't want to start an argument.

POLLY. So he left me. To fend for myself. At a tea party.

CARL. A tea party.

POLLY. You don't think you're going to have to go to a fucking tea party with her?

SAL *stands up and checks on the rice.*

HARRIET. Not [many].

DAVID. I don't react well to privilege. No offence, Harriet.

POLLY. That's my [point].

DAVID. I was going to leave at some point. I did not want to make a scene. You'd got there on your own, it was time to stand on your own two feet.

POLLY *glares at her dad but says nothing.*

SAL. Well, the rice isn't done but the naan will be ready soon, shall we have it as a sort of starter?

DAVID. No.

SAL. Or we could just have curry and naan, I'm sure some people do that. Maybe it's more authentic. I don't understand why the rice isn't cooking. Bastard rice.

There's a silence.

CARL. The casual destruction of a relationship, by way of a tea party. By Pol Pot. A poem.

POLLY. Fuck off...

CARL. You fuck off...

POLLY. Nothing's destroyed, Dad knows that.

DAVID. 'Right or wrong it's very pleasant to break something from time to time.'

Beat.

Anyone?

POLLY. Dostoevsky.

DAVID. Thank you.

CARL *looks at them both, he nods.*

HARRIET. Did you know that was [Dostoevsky]...

CARL. No. No.

SAL. This is what they do. Carl never joined in.

CARL. Carl was never able to join in.

SAL. No, don't say [that].

CARL. This was supposed to be my night, did you know that?

POLLY. I didn't get the memo.

CARL. Fuck off.

POLLY. Carl's bringing home his girlfriend, she's furiously rich, pay careful attention to Carl.

HARRIET. We're not that [rich]. My father has come close to bankruptcy at least three times that I can remember. It's not the –

CARL. Polly's got issues, she hasn't got a boyfriend, pay careful attention – always – to Polly.

DAVID. Okay. Enough. You're embarrassing Harriet.

CARL. Don't tell me what I'm doing to my girlfriend.

POLLY. *My* girlfriend.

HARRIET. He's right though.

Beat.

I mean, to say, you are – embarrassing – this isn't – this isn't how you said this would go.

CARL. No.

Beat.

Okay. The truth is. Is now the time to tell you Harriet's pregnant?

HARRIET *looks at him – aghast.*

SAL. What?

HARRIET. Carl…

CARL. And we need some money. To stop it. The pregnancy. And we can't talk to her parents – Catholic – and we can't scrape it together between ourselves. Is now the time for that?

HARRIET *stops breathing.*

SAL. Fucking hell.

POLLY. Carl…

CARL. I'm not lying. She's found a clinic she likes, but it costs more than the other clinics because it's – ironically – posher.

POLLY. Private medicine – for the few not the many.

DAVID. Of course you can have the money. I'm not happy about it but you can have the money.

SAL. Fucking hell.

HARRIET *starts to cry.* CARL *realises what he's done.*

CARL. No. No. Harriet...

DAVID. What a mess.

SAL. Are you okay? Harriet? Are you okay?

CARL. Harriet... I didn't mean... I just didn't know how else...

HARRIET. It was just a mistake.

SAL. Of course it was. That's okay. Mistakes happen. Do you want to talk about it?

CARL. / Harri... I didn't mean...

DAVID. Of course she doesn't want to talk about it, she just wants the money. We wouldn't want a baby interfering with her career in corporate translation.

POLLY. David...

CARL. Watch your mouth, Dad...

DAVID. You can have the money. You can have whatever money you'd like. I don't have much money but the money I have you can have.

CARL. Harri, I didn't mean, I love you, you know it, it just – it came out wrong...

HARRIET *gets up and leaves the table and then the room.* CARL *makes as if to follow her, but then doesn't.*

SAL. Is she going to leave do you think or just wait downstairs?

POLLY. Some fucking way to do that.

SAL. Because if she's going to leave – she doesn't know the town and so someone should go after her and I don't think she likes me.

POLLY. I'll go after her.

CARL. Does anyone want to ask me whether I'm okay?

POLLY. I'm going after her.

She leaves the table and then the room.

DAVID. Are you okay?

CARL. Are you done sneering at her career choices, Dad?

DAVID. You fucked that up, not me.

SAL. We all fucked that up.

DAVID. It was the one time she became passionate. Talking about how she was going to make money transcribing contracts.

CARL. I should go after her.

DAVID. I think you've missed your chance.

CARL. And she's not good enough for me so fuck her, right?

DAVID. She seems very nice and marvellously rich.

CARL. Fuck off.

DAVID. But yes, you're probably capable of better. I'd hope you to be capable of better.

CARL*'s eyes fill with tears.*

CARL. Thanks. Thanks for that.

CARL *stands up and leaves the table.*

DAVID. What a mess.

CARL. You said.

DAVID. Getting her pregnant in this day and age, all the options available to you, what a mess.

CARL. I know.

CARL *leaves the room.*

There's silence.

SAL *walks up and turns off the oven, then she checks the rice.*

SAL. The naan's cooked. The rice is done.

DAVID. Let's call everyone back to eat then.

SAL. I'm not sure if that was your fault or mine. I think you shaded it.

DAVID. Shall we both accept a modicum of responsibility and thus ensure no splits in our fabric?

SAL. I cooked a fucking meal.

DAVID. And it smells very nice. Almost edible.

SAL. Thank you.

DAVID. And you look very nice, did I say?

SAL. You didn't, maybe you did, I've forgotten if you did, so maybe you should have said it a little more vehemently.

DAVID. Is he going to be okay?

SAL. I suspect so. She might not be. Harriet.

DAVID. Harder for her.

SAL. Yes.

DAVID. He'll get over it.

SAL. Yes.

DAVID. But I hope he learns some lessons.

SAL. Yes.

She gets up and sits on his lap.

Okay?

DAVID. Okay.

SAL. Okay.

TOM *walks into the room. He sees his mum in his dad's lap.*

TOM. I'm interrupting.

SAL. You're okay.

He comes in.

Shall I plate you up some food?

TOM. No. I'm not hungry.

SAL. You're later than I thought, did you go for a walk or something after – detention?

She gets off DAVID*'s lap.*

TOM. I love how you have to hesitate before the word detention, Sal. Where is everyone? Aren't we supposed to be meeting the posh girlfriend?

DAVID. Posh girlfriend is pregnant. Posh girlfriend left. Big posh drama.

TOM. Fuck. Really? That's quite wild.

DAVID. Yes. Wild is the word.

SAL. I always thought we were quite posh. Comparatively. We own this house. Our kids are going to university.

TOM. Only two of them.

SAL. Don't say that.

TOM. Do you want to be posh, Sal?

SAL. Not especially. Just – thought we were. I suppose it's just my childhood was a bit – harder – comparatively.

DAVID (*Yorkshire accent*). 'We used to have to get up out of the shoebox at twelve o'clock at night, and LICK the road clean with our tongues.'

SAL. Luxury.

DAVID *hits the table, delighted.*

TOM. I have no idea where you two have gone.

SAL. We're quoting *Monty Python*.

TOM *gets up and looks at the pots on the stove and the naan in the oven.*

DAVID. We're actually not. Four Yorkshireman Sketch. It was written for *At Last the 1948 Show.*

SAL. Was it now?

TOM. Is this naan? I'll eat a naan.

SAL. Plain? But I've made a curry.

TOM. Yeah. Plain.

He takes it out of the oven, it's hot. He puts it on a plate.

DAVID. So – how was school?

TOM. Triumphant.

DAVID. And detention was – ?

TOM. Exhilarating.

DAVID. I have no problem saying it. Detention. You see?

SAL. Did they let you do that essay at least? I've been telling them they need to start letting kids do homework in there –

TOM. I did the essay. Do you need me to eat this with you or can I leave?

SAL. You can go.

TOM. That way you can go back to giving him a hand job or whatever.

DAVID. Thank you for being so understanding of our primal needs.

TOM. Yeah. Okay.

He gets up, carrying his naan.

DAVID. Do I run away on you?

TOM. What?

DAVID. Your sister thinks I abandoned her on her first day at Cambridge.

TOM. Pretty sure she thinks everyone abandons her.

DAVID. Do I – have I let you down?

TOM. You could have told the school to fuck off. When they were trying to expel me.

DAVID. I was trying to placate them so they wouldn't expel you. They didn't expel you.

TOM. Yeah? You see, there was a reason. You're both fine. I'm the disappointment. See you later.

He exits with his naan on a plate.

SAL. I'll find that plate underneath in his bed in about three weeks' time. Covered in mould and dirty wank tissues.

DAVID. You were sitting on my lap.

She sits on his lap.

We could eat it ourselves. Your curry.

SAL. It's probably disgusting.

He kisses her.

You didn't run away.

DAVID. I did run away.

SAL. But you were mean to Carl.

DAVID. I know. I just was upset. I'll talk to him. Later.

SAL. You're quite a good dad.

DAVID. Room for improvement, I know.

He kisses her again, he smiles.

SAL. Well. You'll be a wonderful granddad.

DAVID. No.

SAL (*enjoying the tease so much*). No? You're not ready for that yet?

DAVID. No.

SAL. Old Father Time…

DAVID. I will tickle you. I am capable of tickling you. You won't like it.

SAL. At least their progeny would be rich.

DAVID. And so the problems are passed – from one generation to the next.

SAL. You don't think we're going to pass on problems?

DAVID. This is hardly a service station kingdom.

SAL. It's something… I read an interesting piece the other day – *Guardian* or *TLS* I think – about entrenched wealth – how it's the middle classes keeping and passing on – that's the –

how it's kingdoms like ours that are the cause of the growing
inequality – in this country.

DAVID. Yes. Yes.

He looks at her.

Yes.

There's a silence, they both contemplate that.

Well, that's a long way off.

There's another silence.

Who was it said it's a child's ambition that truly ages you.

SAL. You, I think. And I'm not sure they have an ambition. Not
a true one. We're safe yet.

DAVID. Or unsafe.

Beat.

SAL. I remember Polly telling us she wanted to be Helena
Kennedy too. She'll get that back. No need for too much
gnashing of teeth.

DAVID. I'm not gnashing my teeth – yet.

SAL. No.

DAVID. Though fucking hell, pregnant.

SAL. I know, but you're right, he'll survive it. They'll survive it.
We'll survive it.

DAVID. She wasn't very clever, was she?

SAL. And she didn't have the slightest interest in the family
business. I'd find it fascinating.

He kisses her again.

DAVID. The lives we lead.

SAL. I know.

ACT TWO

2007.

POLLY *is carrying knives and forks to the table, she lays it as she talks on the phone.*

POLLY. Because I won't...

Because you're perverted...

It's early evening, that's quite perverted...

Time can be perverted...

Of course it can...

An un-perverted time? Eleven o'clock...

p.m....

Because I'm not fucking elevenses...

Because it's more – appropriate to feel horny then...

Seven o'clock is dinner time, it's the *Channel 4 News*...

Emmerdale is on, no one shags in front of *Emmerdale*...

And if I wasn't in my mum's house...

You know I am...

This isn't sexuality, it's rage...

I'm frightened of you not...

Fine, hang on, I'll go to the bathroom...

I need to hang up...

Because I can't take the picture whilst being on the phone...

Yes, I will...

Yes, I will...

Because when I say I'll do something I deliver on it...

Then get warmed up...

I know, I can hear…

Fuck off. Proof's in the pudding…

Pudding…

I said pudding…

Three minutes. Bye.

She exits the room.

After a beat she re-enters the room.

Fuck.

She thinks, she checks her watch, she undoes her bra under her T-shirt, she puts her phone on camera mode. She sticks the phone up her top. She takes a photo. She looks at the photo.

Fuck.

She pulls her T-shirt open at the top, she tries again. She looks at the photo.

Fuck.

She opens the door.

I'm taking a private call in the kitchen. Stay out of the kitchen, okay?

She lifts her T-shirt and takes a shot. This is obscured from the audience.

She looks at the photo.

She's dissatisfied.

She looks around for the better light, she takes another shot. It remains obscured from the audience.

TOM *enters, he's got wet hair. She pulls down her T-shirt quickly.*

Fuck off.

TOM. Okay.

POLLY. I said I was taking a private call.

TOM. Okay.

He exits again.

After a beat he knocks.

POLLY. You can come in.

TOM (*off*). Not coming in. Just saying sorry.

POLLY. Come in. Fucking come in.

He enters. Holding his hands over his eyes.

Ha. Hilarious.

TOM. I'm blind.

POLLY. Hilarious. You should be on television.

She puts her bra back on under her T-shirt. This is hard to do.

TOM. We're not allowed to find that funny?

POLLY. You didn't see anything?

TOM. No.

POLLY. Then yes, we can find that funny.

TOM. Thank you.

She turns her back to him, adjusts her T-shirt.

POLLY. But not hilarious.

TOM. Of course. There's a limit.

POLLY. Oh fuck off.

She looks at him, she checks her watch.

Where's Sal and David?

TOM. Meeting on the canal redevelopment.

POLLY. Canal redevelopment?

TOM. They're protesting.

POLLY. Protesting what?

TOM. They're making some people move, compulsory-purchase thing, gentrification gone mad, that sort of thing, Sal thinks it's savagery.

POLLY. I thought they said seven-thirty.

TOM. It's not seven-thirty.

POLLY. It's almost seven-thirty. I've ordered a takeaway for everyone.

TOM. They said they'll be home by seven-thirty. They'll have finished protesting by then. And probably be quite hungry. They had me wait in.

She checks her watch again.

A watched clock never stops.

POLLY. I need to send a text.

TOM. Don't let me stop you.

POLLY *sends a text. She then deletes some photos.*

Question. Can I ask a question?

POLLY. Sure.

TOM. Is he going to send you one of his cock?

POLLY *laughs.*

POLLY. I don't know. He may do.

TOM. These things can escalate.

POLLY. Yes.

TOM. Why didn't you use the bathroom?

POLLY. You were in there.

TOM. Why didn't you use the spare bedroom?

POLLY. No lock.

TOM. Why didn't you use my bedroom? That has a lock.

POLLY. But it's disgusting.

TOM. It's actually not – don't judge me by my adolescent years.

POLLY. Don't tell Mum – or Dad – about the –

TOM. No, I won't. What did you get? Takeaway-wise?

POLLY. Chinese.

TOM. Nice. Who is he?

POLLY. Married.

TOM. Nice.

POLLY. Not my finest moment.

TOM. But you like him.

POLLY. Like him? Yes. Admire him? No.

TOM. Admiration isn't necessary for sex?

POLLY. It appears not.

TOM. You work with him?

POLLY. Yes.

TOM. Dangerous.

There is a text-received noise.

POLLY *checks it. She makes a face.*

His cock?

POLLY. Yes.

She deletes it.

Oh fuck, will he see I deleted it?

TOM. No.

POLLY. How do I reply?

TOM. 'Very nice dear.'

POLLY (*laugh*). 'Golly.'

TOM. Just say 'Fuck. Wow.' And then follow it up with 'Got to go. Parents.'

POLLY *laughs,* TOM *grins.*

POLLY. He'll like both of those things?

TOM. You looking at a picture of his cock in front of your parents will be like the greatest thing that's ever happened to him.

POLLY. Why?

TOM. Dad thing. Mother thing. He wants them to see his cock. I don't understand it entirely but, you know, that's the conundrum of the modern man no one understands anything any more, I think I'd really like it.

POLLY. Okay.

TOM. Actually, it's probably a paedophile thing, he's probably got images of you undoing your school blouse for him now, sneaking around your parents' back. You are younger than him I'm guessing?

She texts.

POLLY. Yes.

TOM. Half his age?

POLLY. Not quite.

TOM. But close?

POLLY. He looks after himself.

TOM. You're quite a slow texter.

POLLY. New phone. Fucking keys are different. Smaller.

TOM. Work phone?

POLLY. Yes.

TOM. You're texting pictures of your tits on your work phone?

POLLY. Yes. Is that wrong? Will they be able to see them?

TOM. I don't know. Probably not. Bit weird though.

POLLY. The conundrum of the modern woman.

TOM. The modern working woman.

POLLY. And her travails against the patriarchy.

TOM. How's things?

POLLY. Good. How's things with you?

TOM. I brought that question on myself, didn't I?

POLLY. Tom. How's things?

TOM. He tries to elegantly deflect his sister's probing, he realises he's unable to.

POLLY. That shit?

TOM. Shit feels too big. Muddy is more appropriate. The sort of mud you find on your shoe where you're worried it might be shit.

POLLY. How's work?

TOM. Fired.

POLLY. Why?

TOM. Bad timekeeping.

POLLY. Fuck.

TOM. They said they liked me. They just needed me to be there on time and because I'm not – you know...

POLLY. I'm sorry.

TOM. Kind of my fault.

POLLY. Totally your fault.

TOM. Totally my fault. It's cool. I'll find something else. Mum wants me to write.

POLLY. That's nice.

TOM. She thinks I have an amazing novel inside me.

POLLY. What do you think?

TOM. I doubt it. But, you know, she says they'll support me while I write it. So...

POLLY. So it's quite an easy way of doing nothing?

TOM. On the one hand... That's tempting right?

Beat.

POLLY. Yeah.

TOM. On the other hand, I can't cope with the idea of her hopeful face when she asks me how it's going or asks me to explain to her friends how novels work.

Beat.

Because the idea of fucking explaining how novels work...

Beat.

I mean, why would she think I had a novel inside me?

He looks carefully at his sister's face.

POLLY. I'm sure you do. If you tried.

TOM. She thinks I'm Alan Hollinghurst or something.

POLLY. And you could be.

TOM. No, I'll just keep biding my time until I can turn this place into an exclusive breeding paradise for Angora rabbits. A lot of money in Angora.

POLLY. How's Peter?

TOM. Gone.

POLLY. Why?

TOM. Bad timekeeping. And I fucked his friend Paul. Fly away Peter, fly away Paul. Do you know Dad's sick?

POLLY. No.

TOM. Found his medication. Don't quite know what it's for.

POLLY. Shit.

TOM. Googled it but no dice you know?

POLLY. Yeah. Is that what tonight is about then?

TOM. Oh. Uh. Maybe. I didn't think of that.

Her phone text-beeps again.

Another picture of his cock?

POLLY. Yeah.

TOM. Has he cum?

POLLY. Yeah.

TOM. Did he catch it? The moment of eruption? I think that's the aim right?

POLLY. Hard to tell, it's all a bit of a mess.

She deletes the photo.

TOM. Men are pretty disgusting right?

POLLY. Yeah.

TOM. Never done that. Cock pic.

POLLY. Any reason why not...?

Another text. She checks it.

TOM. What does he want now?

POLLY. Asking if I came.

TOM. Text back 'That would be telling' and then a semi-colon-wink thing.

POLLY *does*.

POLLY. You're good at this.

TOM. Just a dude.

POLLY. Doesn't he know I'm with my parents? I mean, logically...

TOM. Straight men and the female orgasm. A bewildered book by I don't fucking know.

POLLY *laughs*.

I think the presumption is that you can just – I don't know – orgasm on the bus just through the power of thought –

There's a text back, POLLY *checks it.*

POLLY. Jesus.

TOM. Can I see it?

POLLY. I thought you didn't like pics?

TOM. I'm intrigued.

POLLY. Yes, well, I'm not showing you a picture of my boyfriend's cock.

TOM. No. Okay.

There's another text.

He's persistent. I'll give him that.

POLLY. Wants me to go to the bathroom and take a picture – elsewhere.

TOM. Yeah. Tell him no.

POLLY. Elsewhere on me.

TOM. I got where you were going. Tell him no.

She does.

There's another text.

It's really good to have everyone home.

POLLY. I'm only here because Dad intrigued me with talks of significance.

She replies to her text.

TOM. And you think he might be ill?

POLLY. No no – no.

TOM. What did he say exactly?

POLLY. He's not ill, Tom.

TOM. What did he say?

POLLY. I don't – I didn't memorise – we have matters to discuss yada yada yada – his emails are always quite nefarious. Is nefarious the right word?

TOM. What do you think they've got to discuss?

There's another text.

POLLY (*exasperated*). Fucking hell.

TOM. Dad could be really ill. That could be it.

POLLY. Or maybe they're getting a dog. That could be it.

TOM. You haven't been here – they've been weird recently –

POLLY. Tom, you know them. If he was dying they'd tell us in a phone call. They can't keep secrets, you know that. This will be something unimportant but important – like Dad's running for Town Council and wants us to leaflet. Don't look so worried.

TOM *hesitates a beat.*

TOM. Okay.

POLLY. Don't get so worked up, okay? It's only them being them, the same way they've always been them, the same way they will always be them.

TOM *nods*.

TOM. Well, whatever it is, it's nice for me – nice to have you and Carl home. It really is.

POLLY. That's quite sad, Tom.

TOM. Is it?

POLLY. You sound about fifty.

TOM. Do I?

POLLY. No offence.

TOM. No, okay.

POLLY. I mean it's almost good to hear you're sleeping around. At least you get some excitement.

TOM. Sleeping around?

POLLY. Fly away Peter, fly away Paul.

TOM. I was joking. Peter left me because he got bored.

POLLY. Really?

TOM. Aye aye.

She replies to the text.

Things get – slow – without you here. Or I get slow. Though I think I need to be slow.

POLLY (*her head down texting*). You're not slow.

TOM *moves in slow motion. He pretends to run. She doesn't notice. He smiles.*

TOM. How long have you been together?

POLLY. Six months. He's my boss.

TOM *laughs*, POLLY *smiles*.

Oh. Yeah. No. To be clear. It's a shitty mess. And it's all my making. Muddy mess. Shitty mess. The sort of mud – like you said.

TOM. You okay, Polly?

POLLY. Oh yes, I'm diamond. A muddy diamond.

SAL *enters, taking off her coat.*

SAL. You're here.

POLLY. Only part of me. Part of me is somewhere else. I've ordered food. How was the protest?

SAL. Why have you ordered food? You didn't need to.

POLLY. Saves you cooking whilst raising the chances of us actually eating. It'll be here soon.

SAL. I was going to make an omelette. What did you get?

POLLY. I don't know. A variety of stuff. From the Chinese place near the post office.

SAL. Oooh Chinese. What a treat. And from that nice place. We haven't been to that place yet.

POLLY. Because it's unethical?

SAL. Oh, everywhere's unethical, darling.

She opens the door.

David, she bought Chinese.

DAVID *(from off)*. Very nice.

SAL. 'A variety of stuff.' From that new place. Expensive place.

DAVID *(from off)*. Lovely.

POLLY. Not that expensive. It'll be here soon. I ordered it from the train.

SAL. David is taking his shoes off, which seems to take him longer and longer these days.

POLLY. Shoes can be tough.

DAVID *(from off)*. Thank you, Polly.

POLLY. And he's getting too old.

TOM. No...

DAVID *(from off)*. Thank you, Thomas.

SAL. Hope you've drawn lots over who's looking after him in his old age. He's not going into a home.

POLLY. You'll look after him.

SAL. I'll be long dead, darling. I can feel the stomach ulcer growing already. I'm calling it Tony Blair.

TOM. Oh my God.

POLLY. I know! Imagine if Sal gave birth to a bloodied ball of Tony Blair.

SAL. Bit too exhausted for that thought.

DAVID *enters the room.*

DAVID. Hi. Hi. Hi. What are we talking about?

POLLY. Mum's death wish.

DAVID. How's she going this time? Heart attack?

SAL. No. I've changed my mind. Suicide. I'm going to set light to myself in front of Millbank.

DAVID. You look nice, Pol.

POLLY. Thank you, David.

DAVID. Fucking hate shoes.

POLLY. Who doesn't.

DAVID. Whoever it was who first thought that the most sensible means of getting around was to wrap leather or cloth round their feet.

POLLY. An absurdity.

DAVID. Am I quoting? I'm sure I read something about it once – is it Rousseau? Sal, is it Rousseau?

POLLY. No.

SAL. I don't think so.

DAVID. And the trouble is we've completely fucking evolved our way out of hardened soles, and built an urban infrastructure around ourselves which absolutely goes against bare-feet walking.

POLLY. Definitely isn't Rousseau.

DAVID. Answer me this, I understand why roads have to be concrete but why can't pavements just be hardened soil?

TOM. Mud.

DAVID. We shouldn't be frightened of mud.

POLLY. Pushchairs. They have reason to be frightened of mud.

DAVID. Carry babies in a wrap.

POLLY. And then there's the issue of wheelchairs.

Beat.

DAVID. Good to see you.

They embrace.

SAL. Did I do that? I didn't do that, did I? And after you defeated your dad so eloquently. Wheelchairs. Wonderful.

She hugs POLLY.

Oh, you smell. She's wearing perfume.

POLLY. I am.

SAL. What kind of perfume?

POLLY. Chanel No 5.

SAL. That's a famous one, isn't it?

POLLY. Sometimes you make yourself sound almost autistic, Mum.

SAL. I like it. You smell nice. It's so good to have you home, isn't it nice to have her home, David?

TOM. It is nice.

POLLY. How was the protest?

SAL. Freezing, they wouldn't let us come inside.

POLLY. Were any of the residents you were protesting for there?

SAL. Oh, darling, live off your wheelchair success for a moment before diving right into wanton destruction will you?

POLLY. Sorry.

SAL. Are those your work clothes or your play clothes?

POLLY. I don't wear a T-shirt to work, Mum.

SAL. It's quite a posh T-shirt. It's a very posh T-shirt.

POLLY. Play clothes. Where's Carl?

SAL. On his way. How much did the T-shirt cost?

POLLY. Why do you want an answer to that?

SAL. I'm interested.

POLLY. You're sneering.

SAL. I'm interested, oh, and before I forget I'm delighted you're reading enough Rousseau to be able to answer your dad's question about that.

POLLY. Still don't miss a thing.

SAL. It's what'll catch me in the end. Not missing anything. I won't miss – shall we say cancer? Cancer seems safe. Some form of cancer.

POLLY. How long has she been this morbid?

DAVID. Started when she hit fifty. She doesn't want reassurance. Reassurance disturbs her.

SAL. I'm joking. Almost. Are we drinking?

There's the sound of a new-text noise from POLLY*'s phone.*

She looks at it.

POLLY. Just a work thing.

SAL. Answer it if it's important.

POLLY. It's fine, Mum.

SAL. You don't want to miss something important.

POLLY. It's fine, Mum, just someone from work dicking about.

TOM *laughs,* SAL *looks at him, confused.*

SAL. Shall we warm the plates? Food is always nicer on warm plates.

POLLY *checks her watch.*

POLLY. It should be here by now. I thought we said seven-thirty. You're late, Carl's late.

SAL. Maybe the delivery guy got lost, Newbury does tend to twirl around. Is Chinese one of those which tastes as good cold, Tom?

TOM. I don't know.

SAL. You told me pizza tastes better cold.

TOM. Why do you hold on to this information as if it matters?

SAL. The wisdom of the young is a wonderful thing. And we never had pizza when I was young, so you have more expertise in it than I do.

DAVID. In the oooooooolddddd daaaaaays.

SAL. And you were right. It does taste nice when it's cold. The tomato carries a stronger taste.

TOM. She's studied it?

SAL. Did you hear he's been fired?

POLLY. He told me.

SAL. I think he should write a novel.

POLLY. About cold pizza?

SAL. Don't you agree it'd be marvellous?

POLLY. Not sure if marvellous is the word I'd use.

SAL *checks in with* TOM, *he gives away nothing.*

SAL. You know, I'm not sure I ate Chinese until I travelled to Hong Kong.

POLLY. When the Japanese fisherman asked for your hand in marriage...

SAL. That was in Sierra Leone.

POLLY. What was a Japanese fisherman doing in Sierra Leone?

SAL. They had quite the community out there.

DAVID. Less fishing regs I imagine.

SAL. This was the sixties, David, I'm not sure fishing quotas were quite the problem they are now.

DAVID. Cue me giving a lecture on fishing regs.

SAL. Exactly, all lectures best avoided in front of the children. Though they do read Rousseau.

POLLY. Honestly, Mum, I mean, honestly.

There's the sound of a door slamming from off.

CARL. Hello. It's us.

CARL *and* HARRIET *come through into the living room.*

SAL. Oh, hello, lovely lady, I didn't know you were coming...

HARRIET. Didn't you?

CARL. I texted it was in doubt.

SAL. Not good at the texts yet, but I got that one. I was worried. I wanted to see you.

HARRIET *looks at* CARL.

HARRIET. You didn't tell me, it would have been good to know that.

CARL. They didn't want to give her time away, but she escaped, so we're sort of work fugitives.

SAL. Work fugitives?

CARL. If anyone calls me everyone has to shut the fuck up and then I have to take the call and tell them she's ill. Really ill. I'll put on my nurse voice.

He slams his mobile down on the table like it's a sword.

SAL. How lovely of you to go through all that effort for us, Harriet.

HARRIET. How often are all of us together?

DAVID. You see, that's the spirit. Thank you, Harriet.

SAL. Where are the children?

HARRIET. Shoot! I knew we forgot something.

SAL. Ha!

HARRIET. My mother has them.

SAL. You could have brought them. Then we'd be all together.

HARRIET. It gets too complicated with sleep patterns and [everything].

DAVID. Sleep patterns?

CARL (*warning*). Dad.

SAL. Put them down here.

HARRIET. They're better in their own beds.

SAL. It just would be lovely to see them and they do love the garden.

CARL. Is this a thing? Is this a thing now? We give you plenty of access.

SAL. Access? What does access mean?

CARL. You spend lots of time together – which is good – I'm sure they find you very inspirational.

SAL. What does that mean?

DAVID. I think it means he's frightened we're indoctrinating them. Which we are. Trying to.

CARL. No, I'm not accusing you of – everything is fine, Sal.

SAL. Have I done something wrong? What have I done wrong now?

HARRIET. Nothing.

SAL. Inspirational?

POLLY. He means eccentric.

DAVID. He means Communist.

SAL. I don't want to be eccentric. Or a Communist. I tried Communism once. I ended up with two different varieties of venereal disease. No one ever washed properly.

POLLY. And on that 'capitalism means clean dicks' bombshell...

CARL. Well, anyway, Harriet is here.

DAVID. And we're delighted you are, Harriet, as a work fugitive. We're delighted.

HARRIET. I'm delighted to be here.

SAL *nods*.

There's a silence.

DAVID. You know, my favourite story from your childhood, Carl. Polly. We were off to some party, took you two along – it was before you, Tomtom.

TOM. Glory days.

DAVID. Polly was newborn, Carl was sleeping pretty well, and we put you – in this drawer we'd fashioned into a crib that could fit in the car boot nicely.

TOM. As long as it fit in the car boot.

DAVID. And we put you in the coat room, went down for the party. End of the night, went up to get you, you were buried beneath must be thirty coats –

HARRIET. Christ.

CARL. Could have killed us.

DAVID. Didn't kill you.

POLLY. Hurrah.

SAL. It wasn't a party, it was a wages-for-housework meeting. It went on for hours because that musty-coated man came. Talked his head off. That was the trouble with the seventies, there was always someone – generally a man – with a musty coat –

POLLY. – and an unclean dick –

SAL. – ready to talk their heads off. The eighties had that problem too.

CARL. And don't get me started on the nineties.

TOM. The nineties were terrible...

POLLY. ...and the naughties...

DAVID. Seven years in and I've still not come to terms with that name.

HARRIET. Carl left Grace in the park the other day. Just walked off and left her. Luckily a neighbour saw, and grabbed her, took him two hours before he remembered.

CARL *looks up, shocked. There's a silence.*

POLLY. That doesn't sound good.

CARL. She told you that?

HARRIET. What?

CARL. Veronica – said she wasn't going to tell you.

HARRIET. She was concerned, she thought it was the responsible thing.

SAL. What were you thinking about, Carl?

HARRIET. I think the more interesting question is who were you thinking about. Girl from work I think.

Beat.

SAL. Polly's ordered us Chinese tonight.

HARRIET. Oh, what a shame, I'm allergic to MSG.

DAVID. I'm allergic to cats.

POLLY. I didn't know.

CARL. It's a new thing.

HARRIET. Bowel problems.

DAVID. Ah. Mine's more respiratory.

HARRIET. Well, okay.

There's a pause.

SAL. Shall I make you some cheese on toast, Harriet? Or an omelette? Which is better for your bowels?

POLLY. Mum.

SAL. She's not embarrassed, I'm not embarrassed, I think it's good to talk about these things. We all have bowels, unless we're very unfortunate. I'm more conventional, Harriet, give me a plate of sprouts and I'll fart for two days straight.

HARRIET. I actually quite like Chinese food so it's a shame.

POLLY. I could call them change the order.

HARRIET. Everything Chinese has got MSG –

POLLY. I'm not sure that's true. I could order something else?

SAL. You're in Newbury, Pol, not London, deliveries take time here. Not so much of a rush culture.

HARRIET. Cheese on toast would be great. As long as it's no trouble.

SAL. What's troubling about cheese on toast?

    SAL *starts cutting cheese as* POLLY *cuts the bread.*

    It's so lovely to have everyone here. Minus the children of course.

DAVID. Yes. Lovely.

SAL. We're so happy you're looking so healthy and well.

CARL. Healthy and strong.

POLLY. The healthy and the strong.

HARRIET. I am intrigued though – as to why we're here…

CARL. The mysterious meeting.

POLLY. Yes, when are you going to tell us why we're here?

SAL. And thank you, Polly, for thinking of the food situation.

POLLY. You actually sort of hinted, Mum.

SAL. Did I?

POLLY. Said you wouldn't cook – said you'd just make omelettes or something.

SAL. I don't really hint, darling, I tend to ask. I've got two cartons of eggs I'll have to work out what to do with now, but the Chinese food will be very nice. When it gets here.

POLLY. I should call them.

    DAVID *picks up the paper.*

    You're not reading the paper, David.

DAVID. No.

CARL. Other than the fact you are.

DAVID *puts down the paper.*

DAVID. Just – moving it. Brown is waiting to make his move, so he says.

SAL. Brown has got old waiting to make his move. He's like – what was her name – the woman who fancied you –

DAVID. No woman has ever fancied me.

POLLY. Are you going to tell us why we're here?

SAL. When the food arrives.

CARL. If the food arrives.

POLLY. You only just got here!

SAL. When we're all sitting down.

POLLY *butters the bread and then do-si-dos with* SAL *who cheeses it. They then repeat the process with the second piece.*

HARRIET. You two work together without even talking about it.

POLLY. What?

HARRIET. Look at you. My mum and I are the same. Particularly since the divorce.

SAL. How wonderful that your parents' divorce bought you closer.

HARRIET. Mutual hatred is a powerful glue.

SAL. I always liked her. Very vulnerable. But strong in her own way.

CARL. Not that vulnerable.

DAVID. I'm going to sit at the table.

POLLY. I'm going to call the restaurant.

She puts the cheese on toast in the oven.

HARRIET. Perhaps better to leave it until the Chinese gets here. Not fun to eat alone.

DAVID *sits*. POLLY *exits. And then re-enters and grabs her phone before exiting again.*

SAL. Catering. Even when you're buying in. Is hard.

Beat.

I had a challenging day in class today. A boy got very upset about *Romeo and Juliet* of all things. We were talking about the way that prejudice builds and presents itself and I talked about that Romany family we knew – do you remember, David?

DAVID. Yes.

SAL. And he'd had some bad experience or other with some Romany people – and said so but awkwardly, and then someone accused him of racism – perfectly healthily – and then he started shouting very loudly about being judged. It was quite exciting. And quite sad.

TOM *checks on and takes out the cheese on toast.*

TOM. You want any sauces with it, Harriet?

HARRIET. I could have had an omelette. If you had so many eggs.

SAL. I offered an omelette, didn't I? Would you like an omelette?

HARRIET. You've prepared the cheese on toast now.

SAL. You should have said –

HARRIET. It felt easier.

SAL. David, will you eat her cheese on toast and then I can make an omelette.

DAVID. I'm eating Chinese. When it arrives.

HARRIET. I'm happy with cheese on toast. Honestly. Do you have any pickle?

POLLY (*entering*). I can't get through.

TOM. Yup. What kind?

HARRIET. Branston.

SAL. They'll be busy. It's rush hour for food, isn't it? Eight-ish.

DAVID. Solid choice.

TOM *gets out the pickle and puts it beside the cheese on toast in front of* HARRIET.

SAL. Okay, if you're sure, Harriet.

HARRIET. Absolutely.

POLLY. I've left a message on their answerphone.

SAL. They'll get here when they get here.

POLLY. Is it time for you to tell us why we're here, Mum?

SAL. Ah yes, we've an announcement to make. David, do you want to clink a glass or something? Do we have glasses? Shall I make drinks?

CARL. Wine'd be nice.

SAL. We have wine.

POLLY. There's wine and beer coming with our order.

SAL. Well. We have wine.

She gets out a bottle of wine.

Only red. Do we all like red? Tom, open it, pour everyone a glass.

TOM *does*.

POLLY. Mum. Concentrate. On the matter in hand. Why are we here?

SAL. Oh, it concerns the will.

POLLY. Morbidity strikes again.

DAVID. We don't have a lot as you know. This house. Some savings. Not a lot. No – empire.

SAL. No service stations.

DAVID. But we've always thought – we've always thought that –

SAL. We want our life to have had a purpose. We want it to have meant something. But above all else – we don't want it to have done any damage. We don't want to have left a problem.

CARL. You've left three.

SAL. So we've thought long and hard about what we want to do with it. Our money.

POLLY. And you're giving it to an orphanage in Africa.

SAL. No. Orphanages are actually – we've discovered that orphanages are complicated. No, but we are giving it all away.

There's a silence, she looks around the room. Everyone looks back, bar TOM, *who concentrates on pouring and handing out the wine.*

In parcels, to different charities. Marie Curie Cancer Care, Médecins Sans Frontières, Scope, Oxfam, the Labour Party – well, we've a list if you're interested.

Pause.

I understand this might be difficult – that you might have been anticipating or relying on our money – after we die – and we want you to know it's not out of lack of love – it's rather about belief. We believe in you and we want you to be unencumbered, for society to be unencumbered by what we've left behind. Inherited wealth is a destabiliser, it damages those without and it doesn't really help those with and that – well, that's everything. There it is. I hope it's okay.

There's a silence.

The doorbell rings.

POLLY. The food.

She exits. There's a silence.

SAL. You're all doing ever so well – I know Tom is struggling a little – but the two of you… I don't think you'll need our help anyway – I truly think by the time it arrives – death – God willing – you'll be past the point when it matters anyway.

DAVID. And entrenched wealth – even in small pockets is sort of – the reason why so many problems exist.

POLLY *comes back in with the food.*

POLLY. Did I miss anything?

CARL. You'll pick it up.

POLLY. She still talking about her life's purpose?

CARL *nods*.

DAVID. And just to be clear – the problem is not the – majorly rich – they've always been fuckers – ignore those fuckers – the problem is the moderately well off. House prices wouldn't be what they were if houses weren't being passed down generationally thereby further inflating the market, and these are middle-class homes, leave the castles to be castles but good homes should be available to everyone and the fact they aren't is due to – largely to – inheritance. Far better to do something good with it – our – 'wealth' – limited but good – we thought a spread was better so that we weren't – so it didn't look like a legacy project – just bits – and get rid of the entrenched problem.

POLLY. It's fine.

DAVID. The number of people in relative inequality in this country grew last year – ten years of a Labour government and it's still growing – institute of fiscal studies – twelve-point-one million two thousand and four to five, twelve-point-seven million two thousand and five to six. Lots of ways to tackle it, but surely this has to be one.

POLLY. You've memorised some numbers for this presentation. That's extremely impressive.

DAVID. I think we should all be memorising those numbers, don't you?

There's a silence.

So – do you understand?

POLLY. Of course we do. Entrenched wealth is bad, let's not contribute. We completely understand.

CARL. We understand ethically, politically, pragmatically and personally.

POLLY. You don't trust us to safeguard your purpose. So you're contracting out your purpose to other more reliable sources. It's basically the private-finance initiative, but backwards.

SAL. No. That's not what we meant at all. No.

POLLY. Whatever.

DAVID. Actually, there is one other thing – if – for whatever reason – any of you were wanting to pursue something that requires financial backing – volunteer work abroad or agitation or creative work here – the money is available for you to be supported.

POLLY. Sponsorship. You'll sponsor us. Like we're running the London marathon.

DAVID. I wouldn't quite put it like that.

POLLY. Sponsorship.

SAL. No. David doesn't – David, we didn't discuss this –

POLLY. For Tom to write his novel.

CARL. Is Tom writing a novel?

POLLY. For Carl to get off his fat arse.

CARL. Oi.

POLLY. For me to do something worthy of my education.

DAVID. That is not what I mean.

POLLY. Isn't it?

DAVID. But the money is there. Just wanted you to know, while we were having this frank discussion.

Pause.

HARRIET. My mum is leaving us her house.

SAL. Wonderful.

HARRIET. And my father will undoubtedly –

SAL. We never thought –

HARRIET. So we're fine.

CARL. Providing someone dies.

HARRIET. And benefiting from entrenched wealth. But as David was so clear – the majorly rich have never been a concern. And my parents think we deserve it.

POLLY. Bold words.

SAL. I'm sure you do.

HARRIET. Purpose that.

DAVID. No one is judging anyone here. This is not about judgement.

CARL. It feels like there's a fair whack of judgement –

HARRIET. I can fight my own battles, Carl.

CARL. What? I thought you were fighting my battles.

HARRIET. Oh, doesn't matter.

She stands and walks to the window.

SAL. Tonight has not gone as planned.

CARL. You thought we'd hug you and say thank you for your clear thinking...

SAL. I thought we'd brought you up...

HARRIET. You didn't bring me up, I married in.

SAL. I don't understand how I've upset you, Harriet, but if I have...

HARRIET. Oh, it doesn't matter, we're getting Mum's house, provided she dies. Which she'll have to do soon, because Daddy is refusing to promote Carl...

CARL. He doesn't need to promote me, I'm supposed to earn my promotions, and I will be promoted soon.

Beat.

SAL. I didn't know everyone was looking forward to my death so much. I didn't realise I was an income stream you were all relying on. Jesus.

TOM. It's not about the money, Mum. It's not.

SAL. Then what is it about, Tom?

HARRIET. Blackmailing your children to be better than they are?

SAL. That's not helpful, Harriet.

POLLY. Dad, will you stop looking at me?

DAVID. I'm not.

POLLY. You are.

DAVID. I don't judge you for your choices, is that worth saying?

POLLY. No.

HARRIET. Yes.

POLLY. I think you've said enough, Harriet, okay?

HARRIET *raises her hands in surrender.*

DAVID. You are very successful.

POLLY. Also not worth saying. Not in front of everyone.

CARL. He wouldn't say it about me. In front of everyone.

TOM *gets up and leaves the room.*

DAVID. And will continue to be successful.

POLLY. What did you expect us to do, David? What did you expect us to be? Actually don't answer that, I know what you expected us to be. You named him after Karl fucking Marx –

HARRIET. You're named after –

CARL. Guilty.

DAVID. We spelt it differently.

HARRIET. But you're not Communists.

SAL. Arguably neither was Marx, but that's a complicated area.

POLLY *looks around the room for* TOM, *she sees he's gone.*

POLLY. – Tom was named after Thomas Paine, I was named after Polly Hill. I mean, arguably you expected least of me – but still – pretty lofty names –

DAVID. Polly Hill's work on the opening up of Africa is moving and important.

POLLY. But he hasn't rebirthed the Communist Manifesto, Tom isn't even close to writing the *Rights of Man* and instead of doing something moving and important – I sold my soul to corporate lawyerdom.

SAL. When did tonight become so cruel?

DAVID. Why is any of this about how we named you? In fact, why is any of this about you?

HARRIET. Everything is about her.

CARL. Good point.

DAVID. And to be clear – I have never – ever – said I was disappointed in any of you –

POLLY. Actions speak louder than words, Daddio.

DAVID. I am not fucking disappointed in you. I wouldn't dare be disappointed in you.

POLLY. Oh, fuck off, we know what you are, we know what we are.

SAL. Now, everyone is shouting at everyone, fuck it, let them have the house.

POLLY. If I was doing work you thought was interesting – would I get your precious house then?

DAVID*'s temper finally breaks.*

DAVID. If you were so inspired I doubt you'd want the house, you'd be applauding us.

POLLY *starts clapping.*

Money does not equal love, does not equal pride.

POLLY. Such fucking shit.

DAVID. You made your choices, I did not make them for you.

POLLY. And there's not one part of you that judges us for it? Judges Carl –

CARL. Okay. That I can agree with –

POLLY. Judges me, for not doing the beautiful things that make the world a more beautiful place.

HARRIET. The world is not beautiful.

DAVID. The world you've made is not beautiful, but the world we've worked fucking hard to make – that is. You just don't live in it.

There's a silence.

CARL. Okay.

SAL *stands up*.

DAVID. Sal – sit down.

CARL. We don't live in your world?

POLLY. I don't want your house, Dad, and I don't even know if I want your world. I'm just your daughter. So if you want me to clap. I clap.

SAL *gets up again*.

DAVID. Sal – not – now –

SAL. I'm going to the toilet. It's an apolitical act.

DAVID. Please sit down.

SAL. Please realise I have rights too.

DAVID. You think she's right?

SAL. No. I think she sounds extremely conceited, but I'm disappointed in what you're saying too, so angry – and arrogant – I'm disappointed in this entire night. We didn't discuss the – sponsorship – you had to take it to the next fucking level, didn't you?

But I'm not leaving, I'm going to the toilet. My bladder is speaking to me. Loudly and profoundly.

She exits.

HARRIET. Happy families. This is always such a happy family.

DAVID. What do you want me to say, Polly?

POLLY. What I want you to say you lost the chance to say a long time ago. I don't expect you to say what I want you to say.

DAVID. Give me an ideal scenario.

POLLY. Fuck you.

DAVID. Give me an ideal scenario and watch your mouth.

CARL. Dad...

DAVID. Because I've had just about enough of being told to fuck off this evening.

POLLY. Compulsory purchase? Protesting compulsory purchase? What fucking difference do you honestly think you'll make?

HARRIET. It's a good point.

DAVID. The point is to try. What difference do you think you'll make in your work?

HARRIET. That's a good point too.

POLLY. You can fuck off for that too.

HARRIET. No one is eating your Chinese food, did you notice?

DAVID. Yes, I expect things, is it wrong to expect things? Isn't it through expecting things that change happens? Should we all sit back and do nothing. Or should we expect change, fucking demand it.

POLLY. Watch your mouth.

There's a tearful silence.

You're demanding change in me, Dad?

DAVID. I'm demanding you care about the world, about what it means to be in the world, and I'm demanding evidence of that care. Because all I see is carelessness. And that means – you don't live in the world I do.

CARL. Has anyone else heard too much of the word 'world'?

SAL *re-enters. She's in an elevated state.*

SAL. The bathroom door's locked.

DAVID. Okay, well, someone's in there.

SAL. Tom is in there – and he's been in there a long time.

DAVID. Sal –

SAL. Tom's in the bathroom, David.

SAL *gives her husband a meaningful look and then exits.*

CARL. What does that mean?

POLLY *and then* DAVID *exit after* SAL, CARL *follows. They all exit, except* HARRIET, *who doesn't move at all. There's the sound of banging.*

SAL (*from off*). Tom. Tom. Let me in.

There's a silence.

Tom. He's not saying anything? He's not saying anything.

CARL (*from off*). He could be shitting.

SAL (*from off*). Tom. Tom. TOM.

There's more banging. HARRIET *thinks and then picks up a pot of the Chinese food, she starts to eat it.*

David, I'm going to need you to break this door down.

DAVID (*from off*). What?

SAL (*from off*). He's trying to kill himself. Break the door down.

CARL (*from off*). TOM. TOM. Mate?

SAL (*from off*). He's trying to kill himself again.

POLLY. Again?

DAVID (*from off*). You don't know that. Tom. Tom. What's going on?

SAL (*from off*). Break the fucking door.

There's a series of really loud bangs. HARRIET *continues to nonchalantly eat. She enjoys it.*

(*From off.*) Polly, call an ambulance?

POLLY (*from off*). Dad?

SAL (*from off*). Do not look at him. Call an ambulance.

POLLY *runs back into the room.* HARRIET *puts down the food and swallows.* POLLY *dials a number.*

POLLY. Ambulance… My brother's attempted suicide… 34 Talbot Road, Newbury, RG14 7BT… We don't know, we can't get in… Because we know.

There's a series of really loud bangs. POLLY *exits after it with a look to* HARRIET.

DAVID (*from off*). I think I need a screwdriver or something.

CARL (*from off*). Dad, let me kick it.

POLLY (*from off*). I'll kick it.

CARL (*from off*). We both will.

> HARRIET *does nothing, just looks at the food. Then she picks up and has another forkful.*

DAVID (*from off*). Maybe it'd be easier with a screwdriver.

POLLY (*from off*). Get out of the fucking way.

CARL (*from off*). On three –

POLLY (*from off*). Now.

> *There's a smash. And then another smash.*

SAL (*from off*). Oh, shit. Oh, shit.

> TOM *is brought through to the living room.*

> *He is bleeding from his wrists which are wrapped in towels.*

Call an ambulance, call an ambulance.

POLLY. I called an ambulance.

CARL. Shit.

SAL. Hold his wrists, is he breathing?

POLLY. He's breathing.

CARL. He's done this before? Why didn't you tell us he's done this before?

POLLY. Carl, that doesn't matter now.

SAL. What do we do now?

> *There's a silence.*

> *Then comes darkness.*

ACT THREE

2017.

CARL *and* POLLY *are wearing bright clothes (slightly uncomfortably). They are sitting at the table with a pad of paper in front of them.*

CARL. You want to talk first?

POLLY. I don't care.

CARL. You should start.

POLLY. You mean you want me to start.

CARL. I don't mind. I just think you should start.

POLLY. It's harder starting than finishing – you're going to be the finisher, are you – that's definitely easier.

CARL. If you want to finish…

POLLY. Thing about starting is…

> POLLY *thinks. She thinks of what should come first. She stands up, ready to speak.*

> Starting is tough.

CARL. I just think – you were the favourite. You should start.

POLLY. That's quite a stupid thing to say.

CARL. What?

POLLY. No need for the F-bomb.

CARL. What F-bomb?

POLLY. The 'you were the favourite' bomb.

CARL. You were the favourite.

POLLY. We're both over fucking forty, Carl, no need for it, no need for it at all.

CARL. You're thirty-nine.

POLLY. Metaphorically over forty.

CARL. 'Metaphorically'?

POLLY. My point still stands.

CARL. Okay. You two talked most.

POLLY. Only because you never called.

CARL. And that's not a bomb?

POLLY retracts her head slightly.

TOM *enters at the back.*

TOM. Can I leave you guys in charge of the lasagne?

CARL. No. We'll fuck it up.

TOM. I have four lasagnes – lasagne – is lasagne its own plural – ? – in here, they're close to the edge but not quite crisping – if at any point the oven starts to spew smoke then please do something about it.

POLLY. Okay.

TOM. Thank you.

He exits.

CARL. When did I talk? Really? At dinner it'd be you and her talking about – whatever – Dad chipping in with a witty aside or philosophical clanger and Tom doing whatever he could to not actually be there.

POLLY. Is that what it felt like?

CARL. Not felt like, how it was, which was fine by the way.

POLLY. Seems like a festering bruise to me that you've decided to let out today of all days.

CARL. You should talk first.

POLLY. Maybe we shouldn't talk at all.

CARL. Dad said you got promoted again.

POLLY. Yeah.

CARL. You're a partner now?

POLLY. Junior partner.

CARL. That's good.

POLLY. Dad doesn't approve.

CARL. Of course not, but nice one. Massive wonga.

POLLY. Thank you.

CARL. I mean massive – you've now got an equity stake, right?

POLLY. Yup. When the firm next represents whichever oil company is trying to cheat its workers out of millions in insurance, I'll get a healthy cheque.

CARL. Cool.

POLLY. Yeah.

CARL. Any movement on the Phil front?

POLLY. He keeps asking me to marry him, settle down and have children.

CARL. And where do you stand on that?

POLLY. Ethically, politically, pragmatically or personally?

CARL. You still say that?

POLLY. Yup. Never grew up, remember? Like Peter Pan but with tits.

CARL. You going to say yes?

POLLY. Probably not, but I enjoy being asked.

CARL. What puts you off?

POLLY. Honestly?

CARL. Yes.

POLLY. The feeling that I can do better.

CARL. Okay. I admire that. Okay.

POLLY *smiles*.

POLLY. How's your work?

CARL. Passable.

POLLY. How are the kids?

CARL. Grace is still not talking to me.

POLLY. How come?

CARL. I won't let them all move to France.

POLLY. She still wants that?

CARL. Brexit Britain is no place to bring up children.

POLLY. Harriet's discovered politics?

CARL. She's discovered she wants to hurt me and moving them away on a point of principle feels satisfying to her...

POLLY. She was always fucking annoying.

CARL. The tragedy is I never saw that. I loved her and loved being with her. But turns out – she didn't like me very much. Or she did like me – love me – or the possibilities of me – and then just got – disappointed in who I really was.

POLLY. You know if you need to lawyer up...

CARL. I've got a lawyer.

POLLY. I mean, a good lawyer.

CARL. You're offering to pay for my legal fees, aren't you?

POLLY. Is that so outrageous?

CARL. As wonderful as it is to feel like a failure by forty, having your little sister bail you out might take it just too far above next-level awesome.

POLLY. Weren't we taught – to each according to his needs...

CARL. We were taught that. Yes. But we didn't choose to listen to it then and I'm very keen on not listening to it now.

POLLY. Carl, she was unfaithful to you and –

CARL. She had her reasons. She isn't what you painted her as.

POLLY. I'm just trying to help –

CARL. I don't want your help.

POLLY. Okay, but...

CARL. I don't want your fucking help.

POLLY. Aggressive.

CARL. You pissed me off.

POLLY. By offering to help you.

CARL. By not listening to me.

POLLY. Blah blah blah!

CARL. And yes, she was unfaithful, but – I wasn't – it had gone wrong a long time before that.

There's a silence.

So what are we going to say about Mum?

POLLY. That she pissed us off.

CARL. This is what we have to say about Mum. She irritated us with her very being, she was embarrassing, she asked questions of everything, she made everything into a lesson, she had the tendency to cut you down to size when you needed blowing up and of blowing you up when you needed cutting down to size. She was fiercely committed to everything and unafraid of making her children's problems feel insignificant. Most mothers threatened to send their kids' food to the starving Africans, she actually did it. She could hurt people terribly and sometimes did so without thinking. We loved her. Let's go get drunk.

POLLY. You see, you should talk first. Just say that.

CARL. Yeah.

There's a pause.

I used to have dreams that I was an orphan.

POLLY. Snap.

CARL. Switched at birth, ever do that?

POLLY. I thought Lucy Wainwright's parents might actually be mine.

CARL. Who was Lucy Wainwright?

POLLY. Ginger. Freckles. Her mum was a dinner lady. You?

CARL. Daedalus.

POLLY. As in Icarus's dad?

CARL. Built his son a set of wings, was it his fault his son flew them too close to the sun? In fact, he specifically warned him not to fly them too close to the sun.

POLLY. Great guy.

CARL. I always thought so. I mean, his son died a tragic death for which he bears partial responsibility. But – give me wings that I can fly, Daddio. I mean, he actually did, give his son wings.

POLLY laughs. Pause.

POLLY. What kind of fucking kid wants their dad to be Daedalus?

CARL. I loved my Greek myths.

POLLY. I love you.

CARL. No. You don't.

There's a pause.

You know that thing they say – that it's not until you're a parent yourself that you appreciate what your parent was – how good your parent was...

POLLY. Yeah.

CARL. True actually. Surprising though because you have all these dreams of the parent you're going to be.

POLLY. And then you turn into your dad?

CARL. No. You turn into someone far shitter. It's a real fucking shame. You talk first. Tell everyone she was funny and a bit dangerous. You'll make it funny and dangerous. It'll be brilliant.

TOM re-enters.

TOM. How they doing?

POLLY. I haven't smelt burning.

TOM. Have you checked on them at all?

POLLY. Did you honestly think either of us would know what to check for?

TOM. I want to have something nice for everyone to eat when they come back. I originally thought – omelettes. In honour of Mum. Bad omelettes obviously.

POLLY. Obviously.

TOM. But then I thought lasagne was better. Nicer.

POLLY. Carl wants me to say something first – what do you think?

TOM. You still haven't worked out what you're going to say?

POLLY. I know, leaving it a little late but late not want not – we were just working out – don't look at me like that, Tom, Dad wanted all three of us to speak.

TOM. I made clear –

POLLY. Your wishes have been observed, but don't – we've still got time to wank out between the two of us what'll be said –

TOM. Beautiful.

POLLY. Anyway, he wants me to say something first. Tell him he's nuts.

TOM. Makes sense, you were the favourite.

POLLY. Mum didn't have favourites.

TOM. She'd have wanted to hear what you had to say first. No offence, Carl.

CARL. None taken. I agree.

TOM. But you should have worked out what you're going to say before now.

POLLY. Okay. Less with the judgement, non-speaking opt-out boy.

TOM. I'm doing food. I did prep for the food. Quite a lot of prep actually.

POLLY. And Dad isn't secretly paying you?

CARL. Pol –

POLLY. What?

CARL. Offensive.

POLLY. He will do though – he'll stuff a couple of hundred quid in Tom's back pocket at the end of the night and say –

CARL. Offensive. Shut up.

POLLY. – for the ingredients. When lasagne costs fuck-all to make.

Pause.

Sorry. Emotional day.

CARL. She's already tried to pay for my divorce and basically called me a fat lazy cunt.

POLLY. I didn't call you fat.

TOM. Honestly?

POLLY. Sorry, Tom.

TOM. I actually got everything together myself, so…

POLLY. Yeah.

TOM. And I'm earning now. I'm going to be moving out.

POLLY. That's great.

TOM. And I know I've been saying that for a while.

CARL. I think Dad could do with you sticking around for a bit, if you can stomach it.

TOM. No, I need to move out.

POLLY. Carl's right.

CARL. Carl also says Tom can leave if he wants to.

Beat.

POLLY. Do you think – is it possible – that when we come home – is it possible that we become our teenage selves again?

Beat.

What would you say, Tomtom? About Mum?

TOM. You've done the cruel version, haven't you?

POLLY. No.

TOM. Yeah, you have, I bet you have, all the things you resent her for.

POLLY. No.

TOM. And if I heard you? If I heard you through the door.

There's a beat. POLLY *realises just how angry* TOM *is.*

POLLY. Then we'd be sorry about that.

TOM. You know the worst thing about my childhood?

POLLY. Heroin addiction?

TOM. You two. Always fucking preening like peacocks, always competing.

CARL. I wasn't competing.

TOM. Showing off. Whining. Getting angry.

CARL. If I'd have competed, I'd have lost.

TOM. Belittling each other. Belittling our parents.

CARL. I don't remember any of this.

POLLY. That's because it's shit.

TOM. History is told by the winners I guess.

POLLY. Now, you're making the day nasty.

TOM. And I always wanted to grow up to be one of you but couldn't decide which one.

POLLY. Well, I hope you've found better things to aim at since.

TOM. I wasn't addicted to heroin. If I was, things would have been more of a mess. And I only ever smoked it, okay?

Beat. She sees his genuine anger.

POLLY. Okay. Sorry. Unnecessary. Sorry. It was a joke – I was actually trying to – I actually think sometimes sincerity is best avoided – particularly on a sincere day.

Pause.

I intend today to be a sincere day.

TOM. How to get ahead in this family – be prepared to say something even more judgemental than the person before you. Not that – I wanted to join in the judging too – I just could never think of a line fast enough.

CARL. Tom…

TOM. I'm fine. I am. Ethically, politically, pragmatically and personally fine.

POLLY *smiles.*

I am. I'm doing well. I am.

CARL. Dad said.

TOM. You're still keeping tabs on me then…?

CARL. No. He just – he said he was proud of you – how you're doing – through all this.

Beat.

TOM. I'd talk about her kindness. How many drowned rats she'd take in. How we'd always find the strangest people in the house. I'd talk about how she talked about things. I'd talk about her anger. Her righteousness. Her unforgiving soul. Her power.

POLLY. Okay.

TOM. And if you haven't written anything yet I'd say that you – Polly, should say something – you're capable of improvising something moving – and Carl – we'll find you a poem.

CARL. Seamus Heaney.

TOM. Good idea. I'll find you some books.

He makes to exit.

POLLY. Has someone been looking after her garden?

TOM. Yes. Me.

He exits.

POLLY *and* CARL *are left.*

They say nothing.

Then POLLY *goes and gets a writing pad and a pen and begins to write.*

CARL *does nothing. Just sits there.*

CARL. Seamus Heaney was her favourite, right?

POLLY. Yes.

CARL. Why didn't we write anything?

POLLY. Too hard.

CARL. Okay. Is that a good excuse?

POLLY. No.

CARL. He's right – you'll improvise something magnificent and blow everything else out of the water.

POLLY. Will I?

CARL. Of course you will, you're brilliant, just like she was.

POLLY. You always accuse me of being more like Dad.

CARL. That's because I wanted to be like Mum.

He looks at his sister.

The only one of us who hasn't changed, why? Because you've never found anyone to bust you down to size. Man or woman, you've always been the cleverest person in every room you've walked in.

POLLY. Not true.

CARL. True. Don't be thick, take the compliment.

POLLY. No. Dad...

CARL. You're cleverer than Dad. And Mum. Congratulations. That's what you've always wanted to hear, right?

Beat.

POLLY. I get – quite lonely.

He removes a piece of hair from her face and tucks it behind her ear.

CARL. Then come hang out a bit with the fat lonely divorcee.

POLLY. Have you changed?

CARL. Loads. Didn't you notice. Oh, why would you? I'm not competition any more.

POLLY. Okay. Okay. I'd like that.

TOM *enters at speed.*

TOM. Shit. The lasagne. Shit.

He aims for the oven.

POLLY. Oh. Is it…? How did that happen so fast?

Opens the door. Smoke billows up.

TOM. Shit.

He shuts the oven door again.

Shit. Fuck. Shit.

He kicks hard at the oven.

His emotion flowing out all at once.

Fuck. Fuck. Fuck.

He kicks hard at the oven again.

Fucking fuck.

He kicks hard a third time.

He takes a breath, neither of his siblings look at him, giving him the space he needs.

Okay, so how does everyone feel about omelettes?

POLLY *starts laughing first, then* CARL.

TOM *stands laughing*.

Okay. Okay. Okay. I'm just leaving them in there – not smoking out this kitchen. Not today. Let them smoulder in peace.

CARL. Amen.

There's a pause.

POLLY. Sorry, Tommy.

TOM. That's okay.

POLLY. I know you tried hard, I'm sorry.

TOM. It was proper fucking Bolognese sauce you know, four different meats, all best cuts from the organic butcher. I stewed some tomatoes from my allotment. I hand-whisked about three tonnes of béchamel sauce.

CARL. Fucking hell.

TOM. No one would have noticed and she wouldn't have cared – food is just what you eat to survive the day – but I cooked her the best lasagne –

POLLY. It sounds lovely.

There's a pause.

TOM. What's the chance of Dad sticking two hundred quid in my pocket now?

There's more laughter.

Then another silence.

Then POLLY *starts to write some more*.

TOM *takes a book out of each of his back pockets, he throws them across to* CARL.

Heaney.

CARL *takes them and starts to work through*.

TOM *opens the oven again, smoke billows out again*.

Shit. I mean, they really are…

He closes the door with a smile to himself.

He leans against the oven.

He watches his brother and sister.

Then DAVID *enters. He's in a nice black suit.*

DAVID. Surprisingly quiet room.

POLLY. Hiya, Dad.

DAVID. Smells of smoke though.

POLLY. Yeah, we thought we'd cremate her at home, save the money, hope that's okay.

DAVID. Fine. Great idea. Like a home birth only more –

CARL. Smokey.

POLLY *stands up, she carefully hugs* DAVID.

DAVID. Hello.

CARL *stands up and is next in line for the hug.*

Hello.

TOM *looks at him and shrugs.*

TOM. We've hugged enough, right?

DAVID *smiles and nods.*

POLLY. Nice suit.

DAVID. Yeah?

POLLY. Swish.

DAVID. Cheap.

POLLY. Still, swish.

DAVID. Less than you'd spend on a pair of socks I would imagine.

POLLY. Dad, you look nice.

DAVID. She made me promise I'd buy myself a new one. You all look nice too. Thanks for obeying the no-black rule.

POLLY. Thanks for breaking it.

DAVID. Black is slimming.

POLLY *smiles*.

Is Harriet meeting us at the crematorium?

CARL. Not coming.

DAVID. Oh?

CARL. She's trying to stop me having any access to my children, Dad, and they aren't coming either. Sorry.

DAVID. She's aiming for full custody?

CARL. Yes.

DAVID. I didn't know that.

CARL. Yeah. She's pretty angry.

DAVID. About what?

CARL. Me.

DAVID. Need any help? Financially I mean?

CARL. I think I've got it worked out.

DAVID. You're a good dad I think, they need access to you. I'd like to help.

CARL. Okay. Well. Okay.

Beat.

DAVID. I mean it...

CARL. A rare compliment – I'll take it.

DAVID. And – emotionally – of course – if I can be useful.

CARL. Thank you.

There's an emotional pause.

I mean it, thank you.

Beat.

DAVID. She was always interesting, Harriet – I'm sad it didn't work out for you.

CARL. Me too.

Beat.

TOM. Lasagne got a bit burnt I'm afraid. That's the smoke smell.

DAVID. Slight write-off or total write-off?

TOM. Total.

DAVID. That's a shame. Your mum liked your lasagne.

TOM. Got distracted.

DAVID. I suspect that will be a theme of today. Never mind. Maybe we could get some takeaway? Sal was very keen on the Deliveroo app. Do you use that? Very good. Tells you how long things will take. Apologises if it's taking too long.

POLLY. Yup. Used it.

DAVID. Much more civil than most takeaways where you have to ring them to ask – how much bloody longer?

POLLY. The modern age.

DAVID. Got a lot of things wrong – but some things right.

CARL. Amen.

DAVID *nods and smiles. He checks his watch.*

DAVID. We should go soon. Aunt Bee will probably be there early and I want us to be the first.

POLLY. Okay.

DAVID. Because fuck that bitch.

Everyone laughs – slightly politely.

There's another silence.

There is something – before we – do go –

POLLY. Has Aunt Bee still got the perm?

CARL. No. She came to see the kids.

DAVID. I've got something I'd like to say.

POLLY. You can say whatever you want, Dad.

DAVID. It's for your mum. It's what I want to say – at the service.

POLLY. Oh.

DAVID. I didn't know your Aunt Bee visited. How come?

CARL. Harriet's idea. Inheritance. Stay sweet. Disgusting I know.

DAVID. Sensible. Aunt Bee is rich. Your mum dying first has done you no favours though – she'd only have given you money to piss her off.

CARL. Ah, well, not my problem any more, Harriet's idea, like I say. And she has enough.

DAVID. Can I read it you? The speech. I'd appreciate your feedback.

POLLY. Of course.

DAVID thinks.

He walks a bit further away.

He clears his throat. He takes some cards from his pocket.

DAVID. Sorry – this feels odd – I might just sit down – read it to you sitting down – take the edge off it, you know?

POLLY *nods*.

DAVID *sits down*.

He looks up at them.

He speaks softly at first.

I believe it's a Quaker tradition. To – instead of eulogising – just simply state. Just simply tell people about people's lives. So that's what I'm going to do if that's okay. Just list her life. Everything she did.

POLLY. Dad, if you're uncomfortable, save it for the service.

DAVID. I want to read it you now – while I can see you.
Eyesight failing, you understand? I did a list. She was born
in Manchester in 1951, the third child of six, her parents
were Irish immigrants. She had the accent bullied out of her
in school. Her mother was a cleaner, her father an electrician
and a drunk, they never had money and her childhood was
not a happy one as a result. She said to me she was always
hungry. She was the first in the family to go to grammar
school but even then had to beg her father to let her stay on
beyond sixteen. She was good at Latin and English but never
found her way with maths or any of the sciences. Every time
she came home with bad grades he'd beat her, for abusing
his generosity. She did well in her A levels and went to
teacher-training college on a full grant, half of which she'd
send home to her parents. Her dad never thanked her for this.
After qualifying she travelled extensively – teaching where
she could find work, but mostly seeing all she could see –
spending a year in an Israeli kibbutz, time in Japan, time in
Sierra Leone. She was briefly headmistress of a school in
Sierra Leone because all the other teachers ran away because
of an outbreak of violence. She did not run because most of
the children had nowhere else to go. She came home to
England in late 1975 after three years away and she did so
believing the values we'd taught ourselves – free love, peace
– had to mean something – she met me, I met her, I thought
she was astonishing, she thought I'd do. She was determined
to change the world. As such she became an English teacher.
She worked extremely hard at trying to provide her students
with inspiration, she took them on trips to theatres and art
galleries and when they questioned why English teachers
would take their children to see art she'd reply that
sometimes to understand imagination you had to see it.
Frequently she'd subsidise the trips with her own money.
Our own money. She sat on every committee she could and
briefly ran for the City Council – in disgust at government
cuts. Yes, even then there were government cuts to be
outraged about. She got pregnant with a child two months
after we met, but miscarried him. She asked me whether
I wanted to try again – I wasn't sure – she told me she was

on the pill, she lied. She got pregnant with Carl and then said we should marry – I said I wasn't interested in bourgeois things like marriage, she said it wasn't a bourgeois commitment it was a financial one and she needed the security of a certificate.

POLLY. Go Mum.

DAVID. We got married almost immediately – they had a cancellation in the registry office and we started trying to make a life together. This was complicated by the fact that she kept inviting people to live with us – new teachers with nowhere else to go, ex-pupils who she thought needed a leg-up, even briefly a homeless man who stole the cutlery her dad had bought us as a wedding present – she was delighted – described it as an exorcism. Still, throughout it all, we managed to have two more kids, Polly and – Tom. When she was offered head of her department rather shamefully I asked her to turn it down because I thought that you kids needed a mum who was around a bit more – and the job would take up too much time. She took it anyway. She thought her job was the most important job in the world – she said the future of the world was going to be remade in the imaginations of the young. We muddled through, there was never a letter she didn't want to write, a march she didn't want to attend, never a mine she didn't want to sit on a picket for, you kids and her moved to Greenham for every half-term. She believed that it was only through the noise of the many that change can occur and she was determined to be part of that noise, and not interested in whether she stood out from it. And she was prepared to put herself at risk in order to do so. When she went to jail –

CARL. She went to jail?

DAVID. You must have been eight or nine. We told you she was visiting her parents. She went to jail as part of a CND women's campaign to fill the jails. She sat in front of traffic until they arrested her. She served two weeks in a full jail because the judge identified her as a ringleader – she talked a lot. She made good friends at the jail amongst her fellow prisoners – several of which came to stay with us. One of whom she sponsored through a teaching qualification even though we – can you spot a running theme yet – had no money. She gave and she fought all through her life – and always had very clear beliefs about what mattered to her and she saw through the bullshit – in 1997 Tony Blair was elected Prime Minister on a wave of enthusiasm – she was our town's delegate to the first conference since the start of his premiership – the women's conference – and she heckled him for his destruction of Clause IV. I thought his compromises made him a good politician – she said she wanted to trust him but couldn't – I think history suggests which one of us turned out to be right. She tried to bring her kids up to be good citizens of the world – she saw them as a legacy project that would protect the values she held dear. She never insisted on them making one choice or another but expected them to follow a path of social conscience and tried to lead by example. She was a good mother – on her own terms – if you were sick, she would tend to you – if you were annoying – she would shut you in your room – she never learnt to cook, she never saw the point. Food was just what you ate in order to fuel your day. But she tried to feed her children on intellectual rigour and social justice. Somehow she managed to do so without too much judgement – something I failed on – as she often reminded me. She was filled with this tremendous energy. She was always ready to do something for others, she was never interested in ego, and she remains the person I most admired. She was too young to be taken from this world that she fought so hard for and I will miss her terribly.

He folds up the piece of paper. He nods to himself.

I failed the Quaker thing at the end. Said what I think. You're not supposed to. Just let the achievements – life – speak for themselves – itself.

There's a silence.

That's what I'm going to say. If you think it's unfair or doesn't represent the love you felt for her or she felt for you, please, now is your chance to say so.

He looks around the faces of his children.

POLLY. It's beautiful, Dad.

CARL. It's great.

DAVID. Tom?

TOM *looks up*.

TOM. Why didn't she tell us about all of that?

DAVID. Not for me to say.

POLLY. We knew some of it.

CARL. Most of it.

TOM. No. Not most of it. Some of it but not most of it. Did you know she'd gone to jail?

CARL. No.

TOM *nods*.

TOM. Well then…

POLLY. What would it have changed? Had you known?

TOM. I don't know. Something. Nothing.

Beat.

DAVID. Is there anything you feel I've missed?

POLLY. I think she'd probably want you to give a plug to Jess Phillips.

DAVID *smiles*.

DAVID. I'll leave that to your speech.

POLLY *looks up at him. There's another silence.*

You don't feel maligned or short-changed?

POLLY. No.

DAVID. Good.

POLLY. Are you disappointed we don't?

DAVID. No.

POLLY. I'm sorry we didn't live up to her.

DAVID. You still might.

He looks around the room.

It takes a lifetime to live a good life, that's why so few are able to do it.

He stops himself.

And she was very proud of you. We both are.

POLLY. Why?

DAVID. Keen minds. Never underestimate the importance of keen minds. That's all you really want as parents – the idea that your young are clever enough to choose their own paths. I think you all did. For better or worse. And I think – hope – you never felt hindered in your choices – which is everything we fought for. Fight for. For everyone to be as lucky as you.

He looks at them.

And she loved you of course. I love you too.

There's a beat.

And we made you. We made you, you know?

DAVID *hides a bit of emotion.*

Just to say – once this is over – today I mean – I've been given the opportunity – in Eritrea – a sewer-building project out there that it turns out I'm ideally qualified to help with – I hope that doesn't make me sound like an imperialist – I understand sewers is all – I'm just grateful someone still needs old gits. It's five years.

POLLY. Five years?

DAVID. I'll still come back for Christmas. Maybe the odd grandchild's birthday. And we can Skype. It was actually something Sal and I talked about together. We managed to cobble together some money for it – so we decided – there's no point me hanging onto this – so –

TOM (*interrupting*). Sell it. Use it for the project – the sewers I mean – that shit burns through money I've heard.

DAVID *checks the faces of his children.*

They all nod – they agree.

DAVID. Right.

Beat.

Good idea. Tom.

Then he can't control it.

He starts to cry.

He controls himself.

Sorry. Right. I'm going to miss her you see.

There's another beat.

POLLY *walks up and hugs him.*

She disengages, she wipes her eyes, she's crying too.

Right.

There's a silence.

Is everyone ready to go?

The kids look up at him.

Then we should go.

They nod.

DAVID *thinks and exits for the door.*

POLLY *follows.*

CARL *follows after* POLLY. *Only just remembering to pick up a book of poetry to take with him.*

TOM *is left.*

He looks around the room. He touches the kitchen top.

He has a moment of pure soul.

Then he follows his family out.

The End.

A Nick Hern Book

the end of history... first published as a paperback original in Great Britain in 2019 by Nick Hern Books Limited, The Glasshouse, 49a Goldhawk Road, London W12 8QP, in association with the Royal Court Theatre, London

the end of history... copyright © 2019 Jack Thorne

Jack Thorne has asserted his right to be identified as the author of this work

Cover image: Lesley Sharp and David Morrissey; photography by Niall McDiarmid

Designed and typeset by Nick Hern Books, London
Printed in Great Britain by Mimeo Ltd, Huntingdon, Cambridgeshire PE29 6XX

A CIP catalogue record for this book is available from the British Library

ISBN   978 1 84842 836 2